EDUCATION, INNOVATIONS AND
AGRICULTURAL DEVELOPMENT

THE WORLD EMPLOYMENT PROGRAMME

The World Employment Programme was launched by the International Labour Organisation in 1969.

It is designed to assist national decision-makers in the reshaping of their policies and plans so as to achieve more effectively the employment and income distribution objectives of economic and social development.

Its main aim is in fact the eradication of mass poverty and unemployment.

The World Employment Programme thus constitutes the ILO's principal contribution to the International Development Strategy for the Second United Nations Development Decade.

There are four major types of WEP action:

1. comprehensive employment strategy missions and exploratory country employment missions;

2. regional employment teams for Africa, for Asia and for Latin America and the Caribbean;

3. country employment teams; and

4. an action-oriented research programme.

This publication is the outcome of a WEP project.

Also in this series:

INDUSTRIALISATION, EMPLOYMENT AND INCOME DISTRIBUTION
Ronald Hsia and Laurence Chau

Education, Innovations and Agricultural Development

A STUDY OF NORTH INDIA (1961—72)

D. P. CHAUDHRI

A study prepared for the International Labour Office
within the framework of the World Employment Programme

CROOM HELM LONDON

©1979 International Labour Organisation
Croom Helm Ltd, 2–10 St John's Road, London SW11

British Library Cataloguing in Publication Data

Chaudhri, D P
    Education, innovations and agricultural development
    1. Agriculture – Economic aspects – India – History –
    20th century
    I. Title
    338. 1'0954   HD2072

    ISBN 0-85664-826-4

Printed in Great Britain by
REDWOOD BURN LIMITED
Trowbridge & Esher

CONTENTS

FOREWORD

This book by Dr D. P. Chaudhri investigates the effect of general formal education on agricultural productivity and innovations that took place in Northern India in the wake of the Green Revolution.

The author uses a simultaneous equations model to determine causal relationship between agricultural productivity, innovations and education. Within the limitations of such statistical techniques, Dr Chaudhri makes a bold attempt to show that general education up to secondary level has a significant impact on diffusion of technology and agricultural productivity in the Indian wheat belt in the North where the HYVs have been introduced very widely. The study comes to a rather controversial conclusion that at least in areas of dynamic agriculture using new technology introduced by the Green Revolution, as in Panjab and Haryana States in India, mere literacy is inadequate to ensure widespread adoption and diffusion of high yielding innovations. Although the findings that sustained rural education up to secondary level is required may be peculiar to the area considered, the study should be of a methodological interest to future researchers on the subject.

Dr Chaudhri's study was undertaken under the Technology and Employment component of the ILO World Employment Programme (WEP), financed by a grant from the Swedish Government.* The means of action adopted by the WEP have included short-term high-level advisory missions, longer term national or regional employment teams, and a wide ranging research programme under which choice, development and transfer of technologies appropriate for developing countries is an important area of research. Increasing attention is now being paid to the agricultural sector where great scope exists for substitution between different factors of production, namely, labour, capital, land and intermediate inputs.

A. S. Bhalla   Geneva
Chief   May 1968
Technology and Employment Branch
International Labour Office

*Other studies relating to agricultural technology under this programme are:
W. H. Bartsch, *Employment and Technology Choice in Asian Agriculture* (Praeger, New York, for the ILO, 1977); I. Z. Bhatty, *Technological Change and Employment – A Study of Plantations* (Macmillan, India, for the ILO) and R. A. Berry and W. R. Cline, *Farm Size, Factor Productivity and Technical Change in Developing Countries* (Johns Hopkins, for the ILO, forthcoming).

1 FARMERS' EDUCATION, INNOVATIONS, PRODUCTIVITY AND EMPLOYMENT

Development prospects of most of the less developed countries in the Asian region perforce depend upon the development of their agricultural sectors. Production in this predominant sector of their economies is largely organised on the basis of family farms.[1] An agricultural development strategy, in the absence of collectivist agriculture, must induce a majority of these farming families to respond to policies and programmes devised for this purpose. A strategy of agricultural development in essence implies a systematic attempt at disturbing the low level equilibrium in traditional agriculture. Low level equilibrium is reflected in terms of low and static productivity, whichever way we may choose to measure it. One of the essential components of the strategy would be a qualitative change in the input factors used in agricultural production with or without prior changes in the institutional structure. A successful disturbance of the low level equilibrium in the agricultural sector would be observable in: (a) changes in level of productivity and acceleration in its rate of growth, and (b) changes in the quality of input factors accompanied by a substantial increase in the use of superior quality, yield raising, modernising input factors. These changes are usually referred to as the diffusion of innovations.

The Green Revolution, as a strategy of agricultural development in the Asian region, was expected to achieve precisely this objective for a majority of the farmers. The use of high yielding varieties of seed with controlled doses of chemical fertilisers and irrigation was supposed to be technically scale neutral and thus within the reach of all farmers.[2] In this monograph we attempt to investigate the relationship between (a) farm workers' education and agricultural productivity, and (b) farm workers' education and the adoption of innovations like high yielding variety seeds, the use of chemical fertilisers and of co-operative and other similar facilities.

Empirical exercises relate to Panjab and Haryana states of India. This region has traditionally been a wheat producing area and the successful introduction of dwarf varieties of high yielding wheat seed during the early 1960s in this region has created one of the notable success stories of the Green Revolution.

1

In this study we propose to investigate the contribution of cultivators' education[3] to the increase in agricultural output and productivity either by a better choice of inputs or by a more effective use of labour. To the extent that some farmers are able to produce more from a given set of inputs or perform the same agricultural operations, using their labour, yielding higher output, they will be employing their own abilities to a fuller extent and they will be using their own, their family's and hired labour more effectively. In this sense they might be reducing 'slack' in the use of human resources. Whether the number of people employed increases or decreases would depend upon the level of technology and the substitutions they carry out. These are functions of the technical possibilities of substitution and the relative prices of the input factors. Some technological change itself might be induced because some farmers decide to innovate and experiment while others wait till the economic profitability of these innovations is established and technological change becomes less risky. One of the interesting questions worth exploring is who are these progressive farmers who innovate first? What are their characteristics? Progressiveness probably constitutes a superior information field and better access to the resources required to innovate. We shall explore some of these questions in this monograph.

Farmers can acquire economically useful information in many ways. In the situation of traditional agriculture, as defined by Schultz (1964), where there are no additional economic overheads, no additional research results becoming available and no institutional changes being introduced by development planners, farmers find themselves in a state of long run equilibrium. The two sources of disturbances are (a) natural factors, and (b) market factors. The farmers by historical experience learn to provide self-insurance by choosing a cropping pattern which will not necessarily give them maximum yield in any particular year but will assure stable yield every year. An example of this is the mixture of wheat and gram sown by farmers in North India. Diversification of the cropping pattern, even on very small farms, is also a kind of self-insurance which farmers learn to provide by long experience of dealing with nature. The second source of uncertainty, the market factors, creates different responses among farmers. The small farmers probably tend to become subsistence farmers producing mainly for consumption and using mostly home produced inputs, while the large farmers tend to produce for the market and try to stabilise their incomes by maintaining a diverse cropping pattern. These farmers also find learning to decode market information economically useful.[4] Thus economic dualism as described by Sen (1966) emerges. We get a set of subsistence farmers, economically rational but having a different objective function (maximisation of utility) and a set of market oriented farmers maximising profits.

Once agents of change appear on the scene in the form of state authorities wanting to change agricultural institutions, regulate markets and disseminate agricultural research information, the knowledge acquired by historical experience ceases to be adequate and it becomes necessary for individual cultivators to decode the new information and distinguish the economically useful from the economically useless. This ability to decode new information may come to the farmers in various ways.

(a) The farmers might learn to critically examine it as 'learning by doing'. This, as explained by Arrow (1962), would provide greater ability to those who already have the experience and who have already been decoding this kind of information and would be less useful to those who are being initiated into the use of new techniques embodied in capital.

(b) The state can devise an elaborate extension system, such as demonstration plots to inform farmers of the new information on inputs, techniques etc. This can be done by personal contacts of the extension agents or through the use of mass media like radio, television.

(c) In close-knit village communities there is a lot of personal, family and social interaction among farmers with different types of information field. This interaction can also contribute to an expansion of the information field of the farmer.

All these methods enlarge the farmers' information field. But the ability to separate out the useful information from the not so useful still has to be with the farmer himself. In this way we postulate that progressiveness may depend on the information field and the information field can be expanded by (a) learning by doing, (b) state effort in terms of extension and demonstration, (c) information learning through social interaction, and (d) reading about the economically useful information in journals, books and extension agencies' propaganda leaflets. We propose to explore the hypothesis that *farmers with formal education of a general type are the early adopters of yield raising inputs.* This is probably because their information field is superior and also because they are able to evaluate this information more accurately because of their ability to read and write. This ability to evaluate economically useful information more accurately and more quickly ought to reflect itself, if it exists, in the use of yield raising inputs and the value of agricultural produce per unit of land or labour.

The choice of the measure of productivity will depend upon the purpose for which one is measuring it. For a study of agricultural modernisation in a country like India, a partial measure, representing productivity per unit of labour, land or capital would be reasonably adequate. Of these three input factors, land is most scarce in the short period. Therefore, productivity per unit of land would be a reasonable proxy for agricultural development. This is particularly important in view of the fact that the land/labour ratio in this part of the world is unfavourable and there is a widespread belief that under-employment and disguised employment is widely prevalent in the agricultural sector of India.

Measurement of the degree of unemployment among self-employed agricultural workers (hereafter called 'cultivators') is a tricky question.[5] The three aspects of unemployment mentioned by Sen (1975) may, in their case, give us different answers. Since the land available to each cultivating household is given in the short period and the household's ability to adjust it is rather limited in view of the land reform laws affecting leasing in and leasing out, and since the possibilities of extending the area under cultivation in districts of Panjab and Haryana are extremely limited, the most scarce factor these households operate with is the area cultivated. Since farmers' economic rationality in agricultural production activity in this region is not questioned,[6] they would tend to augment land by substituting other input factors wherever it is technically feasible and relative prices allow it. Therefore, measurement of the productivity per hectare would be a reasonably accurate index of their level of agricultural development. A change in yield per hectare over time would reflect the growth of productivity reasonably well. The degree of employment or the changes in intensity of employment among cultivators would be reflected in changes in agricultural output per worker over a period of time. As mentioned above, these changes would come about only through changes in the quality of inputs used and substitution of inferior quality inputs by superior quality, yield raising, inputs. Economists study this phenomenon *ex post* as 'technical change'. Sociologists have attempted certain explanations of why the diffusion rates in the use of these superior quality yield raising inputs differ among different groups of people.[7]

Clive Bell (1972) in a paper on the 'Acquisition of Agricultural Technology', written in a philosophical vein, goes into neo-classical economic reasoning relating to acquisition of superior agricultural technology. He points out that there appear to be three fundamental questions beyond the economists' unaided reach:

1. What are the various decision rules followed, and which types of farmers are guided by them?
2. What causes one farmer to innovate when another of identical status, kin, power, etc., does not?
3. Granted that a farmer in a community attempts to innovate, what kinds of social pressure are brought to bear to prevent his doing so? And if he succeeds, what social and political obstacles are placed in the way of others, possibly less privileged and powerful, attempting to follow his example?

In this study we propose to investigate some aspects of these questions with a major hypothesis that *farmers with a superior information field are among the first to innovate.* Superiority of information field i.e., the ability to know what, why, when and where, may be more widely prevalent among farmers with a general formal education. And it is this superiority of information which reduces the risk element in innovation and induces them to adopt new inputs, techniques and practices and they are known as innovators. We may call such cultivators progressive farmers.

If we find that cultivators with a higher level of general education are adopting innovations embodied in yield raising inputs, then we would know that they would tend to create employment for themselves and other working members of their families directly which would be reflected in an increase in agricultural output per worker. This would reduce 'slack' in the employment of their family labour but will not be reflected in statistics of unemployment and employment as collected in conventional ways. This would also enable the cultivators to use their entrepreneurial ability more effectively, because in a dynamic agriculture the decisions regarding the choice of inputs, the choice of crops and the decisions relating to the disposal of the output become economically more important since most of the yield raising inputs have to be purchased from the market and have to be paid for in money terms. This would necessitate cultivators' participation in the monetised market for agricultural inputs and outputs. Larger output per farm and per worker on the farm would also increase the scale of operations in the economic sense even though their farm size has not changed. This would necessitate more intensive management which is a part of entrepreneurial activity. All this would create employment in the economic sense and would be reflected in our second concept of employment, namely 'contribution to production'. The larger output per unit of land may also tend to shift the demand curve for landless agricultural labourers to the right. The extent of this shift would depend upon the relative prices of labour and its nearest substitute and also the degree of availability of the substitutes. In any case, a rising tendency in the real wages of the landless agricultural labourers over time is indicative of the demand for labour shifting to the right. Since we know that the possibility of extending the area under cultivation has largely been exhausted in Panjab and Haryana, so there would be a higher demand for labour only when land can be augmented by labour or other input factors. Double cropping and multiple cropping reflected in the intensity of land use are very good indices of land augmentation. We shall explore these questions in chapter 3.

We find that the generation of employment that contributes to output in the agricultural sector organised on a family farm basis would be reflected in terms of a higher yield per hectare, a higher yield per worker in the case of cultivators, and an increase in wages for landless labourers only when the supply curve of labour is upward sloping and the demand curve shifts to the right. All these ought to be related to the use of yield raising inputs and the proportion of cultivators who choose to do so.

To explore these questions we shall specifically study the following four possibilities: (a) the role of farmers' education in influencing (i) the level of agricultural productivity, and (ii) the growth of agricultural productivity between 1961 and 1972; (b) the role of farmers' education in influencing the use of yield raising or cost reducing inputs in the same period; (c) the role of farmers' education in the expansion of agricultural institutions like co-operative marketing, co-operative credit etc.; (d) the role of agricultural labourers' education in influencing the wages and conditions of employment of agricultural workers.

The first and second, if found empirically valid, would imply that farmers' education induces a quick spread of innovations which in turn affects employment by reducing the slack in family labour working on their own farms. The third would indicate a relationship between a farmer's education and change in those rural institutions which are conducive to innovations. The last one would indicate whether the quality of labour represented by the educational differences among agricultural wage earners has any impact on the level of their wages.

One of the objectives of this study is to explore the question: what level of education of the farm workers would be appropriate if education is found to be a relevant factor in agricultural production?

Farm workers in India by and large do not have formal training or specific education in agriculture.[8] Those workers who have had the benefit of formal schooling have, almost without exception, received general education. There are many meaningful definitions of education of farm workers. For our analysis we have chosen seven that appear to be most appropriate.

1. *Literacy among Farm Workers* (E_1). The proportion of agricultural workers who are at least able to read and write[9] are treated as educated workers. By defining education in this way, we can find out whether literacy alone makes any perceptible difference to the level of performance of the farm workers. We shall study this both at the macro level and at the farm level. We may examine whether, apart from the social and political benefits of literacy, it facilitates modernisation of agriculture in under-developed countries.

There is, however a major difficulty in this measure. Studies on lapses back into illiteracy indicate that less than four years of schooling (primary education in India) do not make the individual permanently literate.[10] Therefore, apart from acquiring some possible mental flexibility, persons with less than four years of schooling normally cannot take advantage of literacy in terms of reading market news, keeping simple records of economic transactions and other such matters. This consideration suggests our second measure.

2. *Incidence of Primary Education (4—5 years of schooling) among Farm Workers* (E_2). Farm workers with education according to this definition may have the advantage of being able to keep a record of their financial transactions, get market information through correspondence or regional language newspapers or read extension agency's information leaflets.[11]

It has been argued that the propensity of lower primary educated men to shift from traditional and conservative economic behaviour to rational and pragmatic behaviour need not necessarily be greater than that of just literate workers or even illiterate workers.[12] Nevertheless, the economic performance of workers with the elementary level of education could be better than those without education because of the former's reading and writing abilities.

3. *Incidence of Secondary Education (10—11 years of schooling) among Farm Workers* (E_3). Matriculates and above would be treated as

educated workers in this case. These workers have the benefit of formal schooling for a period of at least ten years. Depending on the region and the type of schools in which they were educated, they received instruction of varying depth and quality in national and world geography, elementary mathematics, at least one language and in some cases an elementary introduction to botany and other natural sciences having a direct bearing on agriculture. Such training ought to provide a much greater opportunity for progressive economic behaviour than would be possible in the case of workers with education of types (1) and (2). The extent to which such workers are able to shift from traditional to modern techniques of cultivation would largely depend on the content of the formal and informal education they received.[13] Given the agricultural extension efforts, such farm workers should be the instruments of agrarian innovations. They are expected to be early adopters of improved techniques and inputs. Wherever their number is significantly large, through the demonstration effect, the time lag between the introduction and the spread of innovation may also be considerably reduced. In a way they might be compensating for the lack of formal schooling of other farm workers in their immediate surroundings.

Since innovation, allocation and management decisions are taken by the cultivators only and not by agricultural wage labourers we define education as the number of cultivators with education as a proportion of the total number of cultivators. This measure of education gives us three definitions of education which are different from those proposed above. These are:

4. *Incidence of Literacy among Cultivators* (E_4). This is measured as the number of cultivators with literacy as a proportion of total number of cultivators.

5. *Incidence of Elementary Education among Cultivators* (E_5). The number of cultivators with completed elementary education as a proportion of the total number of cultivators.

6. *Incidence of Secondary Education among Cultivators* (E_6). The number of cultivators with secondary education and above as a proportion of the total number of cultivators.

7. *Incidence of Secondary Education among Wage Labour in Agriculture* (E_7). Since wage labourers normally do not participate in innovation and allocation decisions, education, defined as the number

of agricultural labourers with education as a proportion of the total number of agricultural labourers, would indicate the quality of labour aspect. We propose to explore this relationship between agricultural wages and education as defined above (E_7).

The role of farm workers' education in agricultural productivity is examined in the context of Panjab and Haryana States of India for the period 1961 to 1972. This area is chosen because the effects of the Green Revolution have been prominent mainly in this region during the period under study.[14]

Notes

1. Large plantations and corporations operate only in some cash crops like tea, rubber and coffee plantations and constitute a tiny part of the agricultural sector as a whole though an important one in terms of earning foreign exchange for some countries.

2. Income distribution implications, institutional constraints and other inhibiting factors have been discussed in Frankel (1972), Keath Griffen (1973, 1975), Dasgupta (1976), Chaudhri (1974) and Lehmann (1974) among many others. These questions though extremely important are not pursued here.

3. Since in Indian agriculture farmers do not receive agricultural education we decided to explore the effect of general schooling in terms of literacy (E_1), elementary education (E_2) and secondary education (E_3).

4. For details of reasoning of this line, see Chaudhri (1974).

5. Existence of disguised unemployment in the agricultural sector is a hotly debated subject among development economists. In this connection see a survey of the literature by Kao (1964). Also see Schultz (1964), comment by Sen on Schultz (1967) and a reply by Schultz (1967).

6. See doctoral dissertation by G. R. Saini (1973), Kartar Singh (1972), and a paper by Sahota (1968) in this connection.

7. For example, see Rogers & Shoemaker (1971), Roy *et al.* (1972).

8. The small number of agricultural graduates turned out by the agricultural colleges or agricultural universities seek employment in the Government agricultural departments and do not normally adopt farming as a profession. Agricultural education at the school level is negligible.

9. Literates as per definition used in Census of India, 1961.

10. Gadgil and Dandekar (1955), Parulekar (1939).

11. In India first-stage elementary schools have a four-year course in some regions and a five-year course in other regions and there is not much difference in standards between the two.

12. Bailey (1959).

13. Informal education would include, among other things, contact with the rest of the world and information about matters beyond immediate village experience.

14. It would have been interesting to contrast the results from this area with those from the rest of India. But this could not be done because the Indian Census Authorities, in their wisdom, did not permit access to unpublished data on farmers' education for other regions of India. For a comparison of all regions and states of India for 1961 see Chaudhri (1968).

2 MEASUREMENT OF EDUCATIONAL IMPACT AMONGST SELF—EMPLOYED PERSONS IN AGRICULTURE*

Quantitative investigations relating to the economic contribution of education during the early sixties mainly examined the relationship between schooling and income. The theoretical basis was that schooling created some kind of skills which had an economic value. All the studies using the rate of return approach to the economics of education explicitly assumed that the principles of marginal productivity determined factor rewards while studies using other techniques, such as a production function, implicitly assumed the principles of marginal productivity.[1] In any case, it is widely recognised now that income differentials are caused by a number of factors, one of which is schooling. Becker's (1965) study examined the principles which underline a firm's decision to provide training to its employees.

In the agricultural sector, farmers not only perform the entrepreneurial function of combining various input factors but also provide their own inputs. This is particularly pronounced in developing countries having traditional agriculture. In my doctoral dissertation (1968) a distinction between workers' skills and allocative skills was developed which proved useful in interpreting the productivity differences among farmers with the different level of education observed in the agricultural sector of India during 1961. Harker (1971) explored the relationship between education, extension and agricultural productivity in Japanese agriculture for the year 1966. Evenson (1973), in a paper on research, extension and schooling in agricultural development, explored the underlying production function theory for examining the interrelations between education, extension and research.

A summary of the alternative approaches to the measurement of educational impact and their relative efficiency for our purposes is given below.

1. The Rate of Return Approach

This approach to the measurement of the contribution of education and skills has strong underlying assumptions. At the level of individual pro-

*An annotated bibliography of studies relating to role of Education in Agricultural Production is given in Appendix A.

10

duction, we assume that all inputs are in principle marketable and they are combined in an optimum proportion, thus assuming homogeneity of different units of inputs and complete divisibility. This, in itself, is not very serious but a simplifying assumption because if we assume this we are able to use marginal calculus. Serious objection to the rate of return approach is the assumption regarding distribution of factor shares. For the marginal productivity theory of distribution to hold there has to be perfect competition in the factor as well as product market and the underlying production function has to be homogeneous of degree one. Even if a competitive situation prevails one still ends up with the logical 'adding-up problem'. In any case, the use of an un-modified rate of return approach can be seriously misleading, even as an indicator of the direction of educational influence in developing countries even for persons who are wage earners.[2] This would become more serious if we tried to use the rate of return approach for self-employed persons because among self-employed workers the educational impact does not consist of the 'worker effect' of education only. It has two other very important components internal to the production unit, namely the 'innovative effect' of education and the 'allocative effect' of education. Both these factors will not be captured if we use the rate of return approach. Therefore, the use of the rate of return approach to measuring educational impact among self-employed people in agriculture in developing countries like India is inappropriate.

The methodology involved in measuring the rate of return to a specific type or level of education is as follows. The life-time earning profiles of workers with specific educational skills are constructed with varying degrees of sophistication. One can follow through a particular educational group or one can try cross-sectional studies to estimate the earning profiles at each level of education for each age group. One may allow for the probability of unemployment, the waiting period involved in getting first employment etc. The life-time income of people with specific educational level is compared to the incomes of people with no education or with an educational level which is one step lower. The difference between the earnings of two educational groups is supposed to be caused by that additional unit of education. Some economists allow for non-measurable qualitative difference like family back-ground, intelligence level and the influence of social groups which directly or indirectly cause income differences. Usually a fixed percentage, roughly 40 to 50 per cent, of the income differential is attributed to these non-educational factors. The remaining additional income is supposed to be caused by that unit of additional education. On the other hand the direct as well as indirect costs involved in creating that unit of education are measured. The two are discounted by a rate of discount which equals the present value of the cost of education with the discounted present value of the additional income specifically supposed to be caused by that unit of additional education. Such a measure gives us a unique discount rate which in cost-benefit measurement methodology is called the internal rate of return (IRR). If we equate private costs with private benefits we get the private rate of return to education; if we measure total costs which include costs undertaken by society and not directly paid for by the individual getting that education we get social rate of return. If we measure the income differentials and the cost differences only between two successive levels of education we get the marginal rate of return. One can attempt all kinds of sophistications in measuring private and social costs of education and economic benefits reflected in higher income streams. These invariably would improve the accuracy of the estimate but the underlying assumptions which we have examined above would remain unchanged.

Thus we see that use of the rate of return approach for measuring the costs and benefits of education for public policy would be inappropriate even in a wage-earning group in a developing country where most of the decisions are likely to be major rather than marginal. These problems would be magnified when considering a group of self-employed workers.

2. Human Resource Index Approach

A kind of correlation approach originally explored and suggested by Harbison and Myres (1964), is to construct a composite index of human resource development for a particular country, region or a section of society, and then relate it to an index of economic progress like income per capita or any of its variants. As a starting point the Harbison-Myres study was interesting and informative because their discovery of a high degree of correlation between level of development of human resources and the level of economic development was in itself an interesting point but its use for measuring the contribution of education is rather limited because there is no underlying theory which would explain why a particular level of education is related to a particular level of income. Griliches (1969) in a recent study has tried to examine the question relating to capital-skill complementarity in the specific context of US industry. Even this has not made the human resource index useful in measuring the contribution of education to production. Construction of these indices can be useful and interesting in themselves for comparisons but cannot be a technique for measuring education's contribution.

3. Fixed Requirement Approach

This technique for measuring the educational contribution to production was originally proposed by Tinbergen (1961), Eckaus (1964) and later refined by Tinbergen and Correa (1962) and Tinbergen and Bos (1964). The essential feature of this technique is to construct an input-output matrix for the economy specifying different skills as specific factors in the matrix. The skills required to produce different kinds of output would be fixed and given because the input-output relations specified in the matrix are based on a given technology. Substitution among various input factors, including skills, is assumed to be zero. Therefore the degree of accuracy with the use of this technique would depend upon the size of the matrix. With the matrix specified in a sufficiently detailed manner we shall be reasonably close to reality. The data requirements for such an exercise are rather demanding and the efforts and costs involved in construction of such matrices even with the availability of high speed computers is enormous. Even if one is able to construct a detailed enough and accurate enough matrix the underlying assumption of a given technology is rather stringent because by definition the economic development implies a change in the techniques of production, thus making the input coefficient of the matrix obsolete before they can be used as guides to policy.

Trying to measure the educational impact among self-employed persons in agriculture through the fixed requirement approach would assume away that crucial element of educational impact which we have termed as the 'innovative effect'. Therefore, the use of this technique for our purpose is inappropriate.

4. The Production Function Approach

The use of a production function for measuring the contribution of education was demonstrated by Griliches (1964). He used country data relating to US agriculture on a cross-sectional basis and included education as one of the explanatory variables in his specification. Kislev (1967) examined the use of a production function in the agricultural sector using state-level observations for US agriculture. His results differed considerably from those of Griliches. The reasons for these differences at that stage were not understood clearly.

My doctoral dissertation (1968) using a production function attempted to quantify educational impact in Indian agriculture using cross-sectional data for 1960–61 at various levels of aggregation –

interhousehold, intervillage, interdistrict and interstate. In that study I explained the logical basis for conceptually dividing the educational effect into 'innovative effect', 'allocative effect', 'worker effect' and 'externality' of education. It was also pointed out that using the same production function specification at different levels of aggregation would give us different coefficients because at each level of aggregation the coefficient of educational effect being measured is different, for example at the state level one is measuring the total effect of education while at the household level one is measuring mainly the 'worker effect' of education. The coefficients should be expected to differ.[3]

Welch (1970), using my (1968) distinctions of educational impact, explored these questions further to explain the contribution of education to production. This further elaborated the theoretical reasons for explaining the differences in the coefficients observed by Griliches and Kislev. Welch (1970) argues, partly in error, that the allocative effect would be measured if we define the output variable as the value added in the agricultural production function. As pointed out earlier, many of the inputs used in agriculture are owned by the farmer and some of them in traditional agriculture cannot be assumed to be tradable in principle (e.g. labour of a high caste Hindu working on family farm), at least in the short period. Therefore, the measurement of the allocative effect as proposed by Welch is, at best, incomplete.

Thus we find that the use of a production function for the measurement of educational impact among self-employed persons in agriculture is superior to those discussed above for our purpose and enables us to measure educational effect in its various components.[4] Most of these studies use an unrestricted Cobb-Douglas production function, largely because of the operational convenience of its linear and homogeneous properties. Griliches (1970) did attempt to compare the results obtained with different forms of production function and came to a general conclusion that statistical results obtained with Cobb-Douglas specification are reasonably efficient and can be interpreted in the framework of economic theory more easily.

Level of Aggregation and Externality of Education

Mutual interdependence in economic activity can be either through the market where costs and benefits accrue to the participants in strict and direct proportion to the scale of their economic transactions; it can also be a form of mutual interdependence which does not work through normal market channels. In economic literature this has come to be known as an 'externality'. In the agricultural sector, among a large body of self-employed farmers, the externality would manifest itself in the following three ways:

(a) *In the Production Process.* It is possible for farmers to copy economically profitable techniques of combining inputs, timing of agricultural operations and other related production activities from their more successful neighbours provided such activities are of proven success and do not require resources inaccessible to the neighbouring farmers. If farmers with superior education also have a superior field of information they would have proven themselves to be better entrepreneurs and therefore the imitation of their methods by other farmers would legitimately be an externality of education which would be positive, though difficult to measure.

(b) *Externality in Market Transactions.* Farmers with superior entrepreneurial ability would see the opportunities of adding to their income by introducing grading, partial processing, efficient handling of their produce which would enable them to realise a higher price for their output. These techniques of proven success can also be easily copied by other farmers in the vicinity unless they suffer from some resource constraints. This again would occur outside the market and would therefore be an externality of education, if farmers with education are found to be the early adopters of these economically profitable techniques.

(c) *Social Behaviour.* It is reasonable to expect that the style of living and social habits of farmers with a superior information field would influence their less informed counterparts living in the same village and close-knit social community. This may lead to a more effective use of labour and a reduction in man days lost in non-productive activity. These effects also take the form of an 'externality'.

The farmers with general education might have a superior information field which would make them more successful than their counterparts in the same region. Some elements of their successful economic activity would be clearly known and would be copied by the neighbouring farmers according to the description above. This also would be the effect of education though it would not be measurable directly in individual production activity because it has taken the form of an externality. Measurement of an externality is a rather difficult and intricate problem in applied econometrics.

My dissertation (1968) suggested a method to measure the

externalities of education indirectly by estimating production relations at various levels of aggregation. It was pointed out that when we estimate a production function using interhousehold data from a group of villages in a homogeneous region and specify education as one of the explanatory variables, the coefficient of education would represent only the worker effect because higher productivity caused by superior inputs, which have been chosen precisely because of education, would be attributed to inputs themselves. If we measure the production function using intervillage data some of the entrepreneurial effects of education would get internalised and the coefficient of education would reflect not only the worker effect and allocative effect but an element of externality of education also. These production relations when estimated at the district level would internalise the allocative effect completely and a large component of externality also would get internalised. A production estimate based on interstate data would completely internalise the externalities of farmers' education. These estimates would also have a statistical error called the aggregation bias. Thiel (1957) points out that the conditions which would enable us to have the statistical estimate completely free from aggregation bias are rather stringent. Therefore, empirical estimates of educational coefficients with interhousehold, intervillage and interdistrict data would be different, partly because externality of education gets internalised at higher levels of aggregation and partly because some aggregation bias is creeping in.

5. Simultaneous Equations System

Using a production function with cross-sectional data has a serious limitation. Even when the functional form of the production function is chosen accurately, the specification is correct and the variables are measured appropriately so that the coefficients obtained represent true production relations, we still run into the problem of direction of causation when we include variables like education which logically may be both the cause and effect of higher productivity. In this way, the identification problem, in its strict sense, still remains in all the production function studies which have attempted to measure educational impact with the help of cross-sectional data in the agricultural sector. One of the acceptable methods of solving the identification problem is to use a simultaneous equations system and solve the model with the help of time series data. In the simultaneous equations system, variables like education should be treated as endogenous variables while variables like extension and research should be treated as exogenous variables. The outline of the model that is proposed to be used in this study is given below:

1. Agricultural Production Equation

$$Y_1 = f(Y_1, Y_2, X_1, X_2, X_3) \qquad (1)$$

2. Use of a Modern Input (Chemical Fertiliser) Equation

$$Y_2 = f(Y_1, Y_3, X_4, X_5) \qquad (2)$$

3. Cultivators' Education Equation

$$Y_3 = f(Y_1, X_6) \qquad (3)$$

Where,

Y_1 = Gross Value of agricultural produce
Y_2 = Chemical Fertilisers used
Y_3 = Secondary Education among cultivators
X_1 = Total cropped area (Hectares)
X_2 = Number of cultivators
X_3 = Number of agricultural labourers
X_4 = Proportion of total cropped area under High Yielding Variety of seed
X_5 = Number of Tubewells
X_6 = Enrolment Ratios in Secondary Education.

We propose to start our statistical explorations by examining the clustering of factors using Factor Analysis technique. We shall use the maximum likelihood method for factor solutions to measure factor loadings and rotated varimax factor loadings.

Our next step would be to relate yield per hectare, yield per worker and fertiliser use per hectare with different measures of education using regression equations of the following type:

Log Yield/Hectare	$= \log b_0 + b_1 \log$ Education	(4)
Log Yield/Worker	$= \log b_0 + b_1 \log$ Education	(5)
Log Fertiliser/Hectare	$= \log b_0 + b_1 \log$ Education	(6)

and estimate these relationships using cross-section data for different districts of Panjab and Haryana (N = 15) and time series data for the period 1961–2 to 1971–2 (11 years).

We shall estimate the parameters of the simultaneous equations system proposed above using the two stage least squares method of estimation. We shall estimate the parameters of a Cobb-Douglas production function using education as one of the explanatory variables. Finally we propose to attempt a statistical explanation of the interdistrict variations in the agricultural wage rates between 1968–9 and 1971–2, using a multiple regression equation with the wage rate as the dependent variable.

To summarise, we can think of the impact of education, if any, as comprising the following conceptual components.[5]

(i) The innovative effect — this would consist of (a), (b) and (c) as given below:

   (a) the ability to decode new information — know what, why, where, when and how;
   (b) the ability to evaluate costs and benefits of alternative sources of economically useful information;
   (c) the ability to quickly establish access to newly available, economically useful information.

(ii) The allocative effect would consist of the ability to choose optimum combinations of crops, new inputs and agricultural practices quickly. This can be seen to consist of two parts,

   (1) Business activity, and (2) Production activity.

(iii) The worker effect — the quality of labour as described in figure 2.1.

(iv) An externality — neighbouring farmers and other producers in the vicinity who are in direct contact with educated farmers would be able to consult the educated farmers without paying and would be able to copy (without paying) his sources of information, crop and input combinations and related production and business techniques of proven success.

The following chart (figure 2.1) depicts various components of educational impact.

The statistical procedures proposed above are used to measure, as far as is possible, the different components of the impact, if any, of education. This is reported in the chapters that follow.

Notes

1. For an excellent summary of the Rate of Return Approach, see Schultz (1967) and for a critical review of the alternative approaches, see Sen (1966).

2. For example about 70 per cent of all educated people in India are employed by various government agencies and public sector undertakings. Another 10 per cent are employed by universities and educational institutions which are financed by the government. Thus 80 per cent of the educated Indian labour force has a single employer. In such a situation wage determination is hardly likely to be influenced by the principles of marginal productivity but is most likely to be determined by the degree of unionisation and the existing pressure groups. How else can one explain the wage differentials among clerical workers in banks and some state government offices in India!

3. These would differ also because of the aggregation problem, for example see Thiel (1957).

4. This is not free from limitations either. But the underlying assumptions seem less demanding than in the approaches mentioned above. For assumptions of the production functions approach see Brown (Ed.) (1967).

5. Originally proposed in Chaudhri (1968).

Figure 2.1

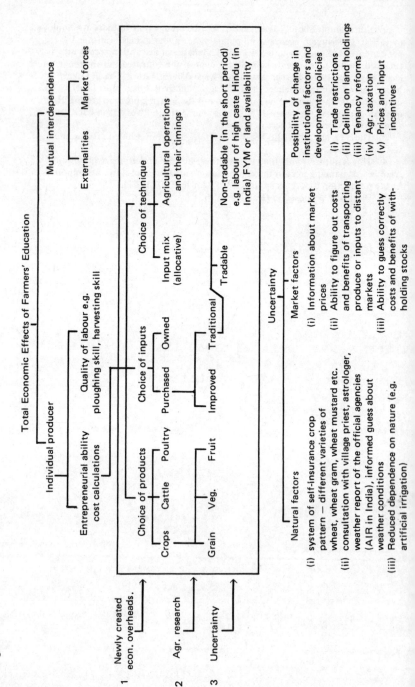

3 EDUCATION, INNOVATIONS AND PRODUCTIVITY IN PANJAB AND HARYANA AGRICULTURE (1961—72)

Output and productivity in the agricultural sector of Panjab and Haryana between 1961 and 1972 registered spectacular increases. This has been mainly because of the successful introduction of high yielding varieties of wheat in this region. The high yielding seeds, when combined with proper doses of fertiliser and irrigation and when proper crop husbandry is practised, yield a much higher output per hectare as against the traditional varieties of seeds. This phenomenon has been called the 'Green Revolution'.

During the decade of the 1960s gross value of agricultural produce in different districts of Panjab and Haryana increased at a compound rate of 16.2 per cent per annum while the total cropped area increased by just about 1.1 per cent in the same period. These growth rates are reported in Table 3.1. Other inputs like fertiliser use registered an increase of 34.9 per cent and the area irrigated increased by 6.8 per cent per annum. Although the area irrigated increased by a relatively small percentage, the importance of the source of irrigation changed considerably. Tubewells became one of the major sources of irrigation. This is mainly because the successful use of high yielding seeds require a controlled and well-timed irrigation supply. Irrigation from public sources, such as canals, is less dependable from the point of view of individual producers as compared to owned tubewells. For this reason, the increase in the number of tubewells and oil engines has been phenomenal and the rate of growth during this decade has been 30.7 per cent per annum. From the number of cultivators and landless agricultural labourers reported to be working in the agricultural sector by the Indian census authorities, the growth of agricultural labour between 1961 and 1971 has been only 0.31 per cent. This is because the census authorities changed the definition of agricultural workers between these two censuses. As a result, a large number of females who were included as agricultural workers in 1961 Census were excluded in 1971 Census. On the other hand landless agricultural labourers increased at an annual rate of between 8 and 9 per cent. This again is largely because of the definitional change between the two censuses. It could also be partly because of the dispossession of tenants forcing them to

Table 3.1: Annual Compound Growth Rates (Percentage) of Input and Output in the Agricultural Sector of Panjab and Haryana: 1961–2 to 1971–2

DISTRICTS	Gross Value of Agr. Output	Net Sown Area	Gross Cropped Area	Irrigated Area	Fertilisers	Labour	Bullocks	Oil Engines	Tractors	Literate Farm Workers Ed_1	Cultivators with Primary Education Ed_5	Cultivators with Secondary Education Ed_6
(0)	(1)	(2)	(3)	(4)	(5)	(6)	(7)	(8)	(9)	(10)	(11)	(12)
1. Amritsar	20.9	1.9	2.1	2.6	46.7	3.4	2.9	19.0	22.5	− 3.5	6.1	10.3
2. Bhatinda	18.2	−0.2	1.4	5.6	33.6	3.1	1.5	40.3	9.5	− 1.8	7.0	11.1
3. Ferozepur	17.9	0.0	1.5	4.1	31.1	1.2	0.0	10.1	20.7	− 1.6	5.4	9.9
4. Gurdaspur	20.2	3.8	3.4	7.0	43.0	2.8	0.9	18.8	24.8	− 0.7	6.1	10.2
5. Hoshiarpur	10.3	−3.6	−1.2	14.2	26.0	−3.6	− 0.8	23.3	33.5	−10.1	0.7	5.1
6. Jullundur	17.2	0.8	3.1	6.9	34.0	2.7	0.1	14.6	24.3	− 1.7	5.8	8.7
7. Kapurthala	20.2	3.8	2.4	3.2	42.4	3.0	3.7	24.6	25.8	−15.6	8.4	4.6
8. Ludhiana	21.2	1.2	4.6	7.7	34.6	5.4	1.6	37.1	24.0	1.9	6.6	12.9
9. Sangrur	14.7	−4.6	−2.1	4.5	39.2	0.4	0.0	33.2	25.1	− 4.2	10.2	9.3
10. Ambala	7.7	−3.9	−3.1	8.8	27.8	−3.6	− 3.0	30.1	13.5	−11.8	−0.2	0.4
11. Gurgaon	15.9	−0.6	1.1	11.8	31.4	−2.7	4.3	38.9	21.9	−11.7	7.2	12.4
12. Hissar	13.3	−0.9	0.3	4.9	35.3	−1.8	1.4	44.3	11.6	− 5.9	7.4	8.2
13. Karnal	18.1	0.8	1.8	10.0	48.4	0.8	1.4	40.4	24.2	− 7.8	7.0	10.2
14. Mahendragarh	14.3	−0.1	0.9	7.7	26.9	−2.9	−10.7	37.6	22.8	−11.5	12.2	14.7
15. Rohtak	12.8	0.3	0.5	3.4	23.0	−3.6	− 0.2	48.2	20.4	−10.2	5.8	10.9
Average Growth Rate	16.2	−0.1	1.1	6.8	34.9	0.3	0.2	30.7	20.9	− 6.4	6.4	9.3

Notes 1. For computing annual compound growth rates for variables in cols. (1) to (5), we have taken 3 years average as the base and terminal value.
2. Gross value of agricultural produce is computed at current prices.

join the wage earners.

The number of bullocks during the decade remained more or less static, but the number of tractors registered an increase at an annual rate of 20.9 per cent during the decade.[1] This would clearly suggest that in Panjab agriculture if there was any 'slack' in labour use it would have been probably either eliminated or at least considerably reduced by the Green Revolution.[2] During this decade the proportion of agricultural workers who were reported to be literate but without any formal education declined by 6.4 per cent. This again is because of the change in definition of agricultural workers between the 1961 and the 1971 Censuses of Population. Probably those who did not qualify for inclusion as agricultural workers, according to 1971 Census, were mainly females without any formal education but who were able to read and write. The proportion of agricultural workers with completed primary education increased by 7.6 per cent and the proportion of agricultural workers who had completed high school or secondary school education increased by 10 per cent. These increases among cultivators only were 7.7 per cent, 6.4 per cent and 9.3 per cent per annum respectively.

The zero order correlations of the growth rates of inputs and output are given in table 3.2. The growth of gross value of agricultural produce has a high simple correlation with net sown area (0.795), fertiliser use (0.683), agricultural labour (0.889) and different measures of education (value of correlation coefficient around 0.50).

We used factor analysis to identify a small number of factors, independent of each other, which would explain the growth of output and inputs in this region for this period. Factor analysis does not allow us to attribute 'cause and effect'. It does, however, permit us to delineate the underlying regularities in the complex mass of data, by extracting from a large set of variables, the mutual interdependence among the subsets of characteristics comprising each factor.

The results of the factor analysis are summarised in table 3.3. Each entry in the table (or matrix) shows the importance of the influence of the factor (or columns) on the variables (rows). More specifically, the square of each entry or factor loading in the matrix represents the percentage of the total unit variance of each variable which is explained by each factor. The first row of the table, for example, shows that 50.9 per cent of the variation is explained by the first factor. The economic characteristics, which have the highest loadings in factor 1, are the gross value of agriculture produce, use of chemical fertilisers, use of human labour, growth of tractors and the education of farm

Table 3.2: Agricultural Inputs and Outputs in Panjab and Haryana 1961–72
Growth Rates : Correlation Matrix   (N = 15)

Variable	GAP	Net Sown Area	Total Cropped Area	Irrigated Area	Fertiliser	Agr. Labour	Bullocks	Oil engines & Electric Pumps	Tractors	Ed_1	Ed_2	Ed_3	Ed_4	Ed_5	Ed_6
GAP		0.795	0.870	-0.398	0.683	0.889	0.470	-0.273	0.401	0.510	0.541	0.517	0.492	0.458	0.499
Net Sown Area			0.868	-0.384	0.492	0.607	0.309	-0.218	0.328	0.165	0.388	0.337	0.137	0.304	0.317
Total Cropped Area				-0.215	0.411	0.745	0.322	-0.199	0.367	0.488	0.415	0.561	0.444	0.322	0.538
Irrigated Area					-0.259	-0.423	0.138	0.114	-0.259	-0.244	-0.381	-0.067	-0.292	-0.393	-0.099
Fertiliser						0.657	0.499	-0.221	0.328	0.260	0.379	0.072	0.224	0.280	0.040
Agr. Labour							0.455	-0.376	0.251	0.670	0.350	0.252	0.635	0.240	0.229
Bullocks								-0.081	0.043	0.201	-0.120	-0.098	0.157	-0.161	-0.114
Oil Engines & Electric Pumps									-0.374	-0.282	0.159	0.235	-0.223	0.282	0.281
Tractors										-0.027	0.409	0.237	-0.100	0.270	0.212
Literacy (E_1)											0.070	0.411	0.987	0.044	0.388
Primary Education (E_2)												0.598	0.112	0.976	0.639
High School Education (E_3)													0.436	0.636	0.992
Literacy of Cultivators (E_4)														0.114	0.428
Primary Ed. of Cultivators (E_5)															0.692
High School Ed. of Cultivators (E_6)															

Table 3.3: Main Variable Clusters Based on Factor Score Coefficients from Factor Analysis and Rotated Varimax Factor Analysis (Growth of Input Output — Interdistrict Data for Panjab and Haryana)   (N = 15)

Variables	Factors			Rotated Factors		
	F_1	F_2	F_3	F_1	F_2	F_3
1. Gross Agr. Produce	0.983	−0.048	−0.017	0.545	0.262	0.204
2. Net Sown Area	0.850	−0.109	−0.092	0.918	0.110	0.141
3. Total Cropped Area	0.891	−0.284	−0.018	0.781	0.151	0.162
4. Irrigated Area	−0.434	−0.244	0.699	−0.154	−0.038	0.059
5. Fertilisers	0.715	0.388	0.259	0.216	0.249	0.166
6. Labour	0.878	0.183	−0.066	0.361	0.211	0.088
7. Bullocks	0.502	0.621	0.211	0.152	0.948	−0.009
8. Tractors	0.431	−0.344	0.628	0.169	−0.006	0.967
9. Education (E_6)	0.433	−0.728	−0.207	0.208	−0.087	0.086
% Variance explained by Factors	50.9	15.2	11.7			
Cumulative % Variance explained by Factors	50.9	66.1	77.8			

workers. Between them these factors explain 50.9 per cent of the total variation. The absence of extension or research variables in this factor analysis ought to be conspicuous. This is because we could not find a meaningful yardstick to measure either the research effort or results which lead to the Green Revolution or the extent of the extension effort in different parts of this region. The extension effort in different parts of this region have been more or less uniform since 1961, according to certain administrative procedures. Factor 2 is able to explain another 15 per cent while factor 3 explains 11.7 per cent. It still gives us a total explanation of 78 per cent of the variation. Obviously the research and extension effort is a very important factor in the context of the region we are examining, and we have not been able to measure it.

Using factor analysis we find that the growth of agricultural produce has moved along with the growth of other newly introduced input factors and education is strongly related with these factors. Our main interest is in identifying causation. To separate the effect of education, we used a regression model in which the compound annual rate of growth of agricultural produce was regressed against total cropped area, irrigated area, fertilisers, labour, use of tubewells and tractors using a multiple linear regression equation of the following type:

$$\text{Growth of GAP} = b_0 + b_1 x_1 + b_2 x_2 + b_3 x_3 + b_4 x_4 + b_5 x_5$$
$$(1961-72) \qquad + b_6 x_6 + b_7 x_7 \qquad\qquad (3.1)$$

where,

x_1 = growth in total cropped area
x_2 = growth in area irrigated
x_3 = growth in use of chemical fertilisers
x_4 = growth in agricultural labour force
x_5 = growth in bullock power
x_6 = growth in number of oil engines
x_7 = growth in number of tractors
x_8 = growth in education measured in two alternative ways
      (E_5) and (E_6).

The estimated coefficients of the regression equation are reported in table 3.4.[3] If one assumes that these factors were independent of each other — an assumption which is implicit in use of multiple regression technique — we find that about 86 per cent of the growth of agricultural output is explained by the growth of various input factors

Table 3.4: Explanation of the Growth of Gross Value of Agriculture Produce through Growth of Input Factors (Districts of Panjab and Haryana : 1961–72) (N = 15)

Dependent Variable: GAP				Proportion of Cultivators with					
	Without Education			Completed Primary Education (E_5)			Completed Secondary Education (E_6)		
Explanatory Variables	Co-eff.	t. Value	Elasticity	Co-eff.	t. Value	Elasticity	Co-eff.	t. Value	Elasticity
(0)	(1)	(2)	(3)	(4)	(5)	(6)	(7)	(8)	(9)
1. Total Cropped Area	0.925	2.970	0.065	0.818	3.063	0.057	0.575	2.089	0.040
2. Irrigated Area	−0.133	1.017	−0.055	−0.055	0.068	−0.109	−0.109	1.088	−0.045
3. Fertilisers	0.101	1.346	0.217	0.063	0.953	0.136	0.110	1.927	0.237
4. Labour	0.414	1.522	0.008	0.404	1.770	0.008	0.418	2.026	0.008
5. Bullocks	0.063	0.486	0.001	0.184	1.471	0.002	0.147	1.412	0.002
6. Oil Engines	0.014	0.353	0.027	−0.034	0.831	−0.064	−0.028	0.815	−0.053
7. Tractors	0.077	0.829	0.099	0.010	0.117	0.013	0.040	0.561	0.052
8. Education				0.336	1.985	0.132	0.301	2.485	0.172
$\bar{R}^2$		0.861			0.902			0.920	

and about 6 to 7 per cent of the growth of output is explained by growth of education. The remaining 14 per cent of the growth of agricultural output is not explained by the factors included in the multiple regressions. This is partly contributed by high yielding seeds and partly by factors which are not included in the regressions; also there must be some interaction of the factors included in the regressions. The interesting point that emerges from this statistical exercise is that the growth of output seems to be related to the growth of education.[4] One can legitimately question the assumption of independence of the various input factors contributing to the growth of gross agricultural produce. We have examined this question using factor analysis. We know that a large part of this growth is due to a major breakthrough in agricultural research, namely the discovery and use of High Yielding Variety (HYV) seeds, but it would be wrong to restrict examination only to the growth rates of input factors. It is necessary to look for the factor or factors that have influenced the rate of adoption of HYV seeds. However our attempted regression analysis suggests that the contribution of education alone, if we believe the direction of causation hypothesised in the regression model, in this region is of the order of about 6 per cent, for secondary education. The contribution of primary education alone seems to be about 4 per cent of the total growth of the value of agricultural produce.

Interdistrict variability in yield per hectare, use of chemical fertiliser per hectare and the proportion of area under HYV seeds between 1961 and 1972 has not remained stable as is clear from the computed coefficients of variation reported in table 3.5. Variability in the use of chemical fertiliser per hectare, though declining, is still very high. This is also true of the area under HYV seed.

As explained in chapter 1, educational impact, if it exists, conceptually could be divided into four components: innovative effect, allocative effect, worker effect and externality of education. Nelson and Phelps (1966) have argued that education's contribution to economic growth is essentially in its innovative effects. Chaudhri (1968) acknowledged that innovation is one of the major components of educational effects but did not specifically measure it since he did not have access to time series data. Herdt (1971) compared the statistical results of Chaudhri's study (1968) which related to cross section data for Indian agriculture for the year 1961 with those of other researchers and rightly concluded that educational effect in Indian agriculture, though positive and highly significant, was relatively small (in 1961) as compared to the educational effect in developed countries like the USA

Table 3.5: Univariate Statistics for Yield, Fertiliser Use and Education: Interdistrict Data for Panjab and Haryana (N = 15)

	Yield in Rupees Hectare		Yield in Rupees Worker		Fertilisers in Kg Hectare		Secondary Education Among Farm Workers		Cultivators		HYV	
	Means	Co-eff. of Variance	Means	Co-eff. of Variance	Means	Co-eff. of Variance	Means	Co-eff. of Variance	Means	Co-eff. of Variance	Means	Co-eff. of Variance
Year												
(0)	(1)	(2)	(3)	(4)	(5)	(6)	(7)	(8)	(9)	(10)	(11)	(12)
1961	530.4	27.2	724.5	27.1	3.1	96.5	3171.4	36.5	3114.5	36.4	NA	NA
1962	533.2	28.6	710.9	21.6	5.5	91.2	3477.6	35.9	3390.0	35.8	NA	NA
1963	665.1	37.4	915.8	29.3	8.1	72.3	3817.3	35.5	3693.2	35.3	NA	NA
1964	968.7	37.8	1206.9	30.7	15.5	69.8	4190.8	35.3	4026.8	35.0	NA	NA
1965	885.3	39.3	1136.5	30.4	15.8	85.4	4605.4	35.2	4394.3	34.9	NA	NA
1966	1389.4	40.6	1740.7	28.5	17.9	89.2	5064.7	35.3	4798.8	35.0	NA	NA
1967	1660.9	39.2	2114.3	26.9	36.0	75.3	5573.3	35.5	5244.4	35.1	NA	NA
1968	1707.5	45.8	2144.4	34.2	53.8	77.7	6137.2	35.8	5736.0	35.5	102.5	66.5
1969	1900.5	36.4	2517.9	23.2	48.6	72.7	6762.3	36.2	6277.8	35.9	142.6	59.5
1970	1895.2	40.3	2364.6	23.9	62.7	74.3	7455.9	36.8	6876.8	36.4	173.1	53.9
1971	2097.8	40.2	2601.7	21.8	77.0	75.4	8221.1	37.4	7539.6	36.9	195.4	51.7

The major breakthrough in wheat production caused by the introduction of dwarf Mexican varieties of wheat and their variants, usually called the High Yielding Varieties, in the wheat belt of North India during the mid-sixties was singularly successful. One of the objectives of the present study is to examine whether the education of the farm workers had any role in the rate of adoption of the new technology which came in with the introduction of the High Yielding Varieties of Wheat and its effect on growth of agricultural productivity. We attempted to study this through a detailed analysis of data for 15 administrative districts of Panjab and Haryana for the period of 11 years from 1961 to 1972.

We postulate the relationship[5] between yield per hectare and education defined in six alternative ways by estimating a regression equation of the following type:

$$\text{Log Yield/Hectare}_t = \text{Log } b_{0t} + b_{1t} \text{ Log Education}$$
$$t = 1961 \ldots 1972 \qquad (3.2)$$

using fifteen interdistrict observations from Panjab and Haryana. This equation was estimated for all the eleven years separately from 1961 to 1972. The coefficients, with six alternative measures of education, are reported in table 3.6. An examination of the estimated statistics (b coefficients, their t-Value and $\bar{R}^2$) indicates that with our first definition of education, viz., literacy without any formal education (E_1), for none of the years the coefficient is statistically significant. With our second definition of education viz., proportion of agricultural workers with completed primary education (E_2), we find that b coefficients are positive for all the years, are statistically significant at the 1 per cent level for the years 1961 to 1966 and are not significantly different from zero for the years 1967 onwards. The result is highly interesting because we know that adoption of high yielding variety (HYV) seeds became widespread in Panjab and Haryana around that period. Is it because the traditional varieties require the 'allocative' and the 'worker' ability which primary education adequately provided for the technology prevalent before the Green Revolution, while the introduction of the HYV seeds requires 'innovative', 'allocative' and 'worker' abilities which primary education does not provide adequately? This question is partially answered when we look at the b coefficients of the estimated equation with our third definition of education, viz., the proportion of agricultural workers with completed secondary education (E_3): b coefficients with this definition are positive and in numerical value seem to be increasing from 1962 onwards. The

Table 3.6: Relationship between Yield Per Hectare and Education: Interdistrict Data for Panjab and Haryana (N = 15)
Log yield/Hec. = Log b_0 + b_1 Log Ed

Year	Education 1			Education 2			Education 3			Education 4			Education 5			Education 6		
	b co-eff.	T. Value	$\bar{R}^2$	b co-eff.	T. Value	$\bar{R}^2$	b co-eff.	T. Value	$\bar{R}^2$	b co-eff.	T. Value	$\bar{R}^2$	b co-eff.	T. Value	$\bar{R}^2$	b co-eff.	T. Value	$\bar{R}^2$
1961	−0.051	0.2	0.151	0.417	2.7	0.261	0.304	3.1	0.342	−0.421	1.4	0.006	0.391	2.0	0.109	0.359	3.0	0.321
1962	−0.138	0.5	0.136	0.554	3.4	0.392	0.429	4.8	0.586	−0.494	1.6	0.043	0.543	2.6	0.238	0.501	4.8	0.584
1963	−0.353	0.8	0.099	0.787	2.9	0.306	0.683	5.2	0.628	−0.720	1.7	0.064	0.787	2.4	0.197	0.783	5.4	0.645
1964	−0.169	0.4	0.139	0.711	2.5	0.214	0.699	5.4	0.645	−0.417	1.1	0.063	0.706	2.0	0.126	0.777	5.5	0.657
1965	−0.240	0.6	0.122	0.603	1.8	0.073	0.664	3.8	0.458	−0.381	1.0	0.069	0.637	1.6	0.042	0.734	4.1	0.492
1966	−0.101	0.3	0.147	0.689	2.1	0.142	0.740	4.9	0.598	−0.220	0.6	0.118	0.756	2.0	0.121	0.798	5.3	0.636
1967	0.090	0.3	0.144	0.326	1.0	0.066	0.517	3.1	0.328	0.026	0.1	0.153	0.381	1.1	0.063	0.564	3.4	0.383
1968	0.111	0.3	0.148	0.315	0.6	0.125	0.873	3.0	0.319	0.038	0.1	0.153	0.396	0.6	0.120	0.939	3.3	0.377
1969	0.170	0.7	0.107	−0.033	0.1	0.153	0.424	2.0	0.127	0.132	0.6	0.123	0.009	0.3	0.154	0.473	2.4	0.196
1970	0.133	0.5	0.128	0.061	0.2	0.152	0.611	2.7	0.263	0.098	0.4	0.139	0.138	0.3	0.146	0.664	3.2	0.353
1971	0.179	0.7	0.107	−0.133	0.3	0.146	0.579	2.2	0.162	0.145	0.6	0.120	−0.097	0.2	0.151	0.636	2.6	0.244

coefficients for all the years from 1961 to 1972 are significant at the 1 per cent level. This suggests that in all probability, the 'innovative effect' of education is very important and is provided by secondary school education i.e. 10–11 years of conventional schooling in this region for the level of technology embodied in the use of HYV seeds.

Since the decision to use HYV seeds and the other inputs which come with it as a package lies with the cultivators only, and not with all the agricultural workers, we have defined E_4 as the proportion of cultivators who were able to read and write without any formal education. The b coefficients of E_4 had a pattern very similar to those of E_1 and were not significantly different from zero for all the years. Using the proportion of cultivators with completed elementary education, (E_5) as an explanatory variable, we obtained coefficients which are similar to those of E_2. Until 1966 the b coefficients are positive and significant at the 1 per cent level and are not significantly different from zero for 1967 and after 1967. Education (E_6) was defined as the proportion of cultivators who had completed secondary education. The b coefficients for E_6 are positive and statistically significant at the 1 per cent level for each of the years from 1961 to 1972. When we compare the b coefficients of E_6 (cultivators with high school education) with those of E_3 (all agricultural workers with high school education), two points emerge:

1. the b coefficients[6] of E_6 are somewhat larger for all the years and are more stable over the years, and
2. the value of $\bar{R}^2$ with E_6 is somewhat higher as compared to the value of $\bar{R}^2$ with E_3.

This suggests that the level of yield per hectare has not moved with variation in E_1 (literacy among all farmer workers) and E_4 (literacy among cultivators) while it has varied with variations in E_2 (elementary education among all farm workers) and E_5 (elementary education among cultivators) for each of the years between 1961 and 1966 but not thereafter. Yield per hectare has moved with E_3 (secondary education among farm workers) and E_6 (secondary education among cultivators) for each of the years between 1961 and 1972 in different districts of Panjab and Haryana. In the subsequent sections of this chapter and the rest of the study we shall restrict our close examination of the relationship between education and agricultural productivity to only four definitions of education, E_2, E_3, E_5 and E_6, because E_1 and E_4 (literacy) alone do not seem to explain productivity differences in

Panjab and Haryana.

We know that one of the important requirements of use of HYV seeds has been use of chemical fertilisers. Since data are not available for the area under HYV of wheat which received recommended doses of fertilisers it would be misleading to examine just acreage reported to be under HYV.[7] Many farmers, in the initial trials, experimented with the use of HYV seeds by combining it with less than recommended doses of other inputs like fertilisers. Therefore, statistics of area under HYV seeds would not adequately reflect the benefits of the use of high yielding varieties seed. On the other hand, use of chemical fertilisers would be closely related to the use of HYV seeds of wheat in Panjab and Haryana for the period under examination. Therefore, we decided to examine if, in different districts of Panjab and Haryana, use of chemical fertilisers per hectare varied with the level of education defined in four alternative ways by estimating the following equation using 15 interdistrict observations from Panjab and Haryana for each of the years from 1961 to 1972:

$$\text{Log Fertiliser/Hectare}_t = \text{Log } b_{0t} + b_{1t} \text{ Log } Ed_t$$
$$t = 1961 \ldots 1972 \qquad (3.3)$$

The b coefficients, t-Value and $\bar{R}^2$ with each of the six alternative definitions of education for the years 1961 to 1972 are reported in table 3.7. The pattern of the relationship between the use of chemical fertiliser per hectare and education is very similar to that observed while examining the relationships between yield per hectare and education. The coefficients of education for E_1 and E_4 are not significantly different from zero for all the years from 1961 to 1972. The coefficient of E_2 is positive and statistically significant at the 1 per cent level for each of the years from 1961 to 1966 but becomes statistically insignificant for the years after 1966. The coefficient of E_5 also follows the same pattern, i.e., it is positive and statistically significant for each of the years between 1961 and 1966 and is not significantly different from zero thereafter. The coefficient of E_3 is positive and significant at the 1 per cent level for each year between 1961 and 1972. The coefficient of E_6 also is positive and statistically significant for each of these years. A comparison between the coefficients and E_3 and E_6 indicates that the numerical value of the coefficient of E_6 is somewhat larger for all the years as could have been expected. We know that the use of chemical fertilisers dur-ing this decade in Panjab and Haryana has been closely linked with the

Table 3.7: Relationship between Fertiliser per Hectare and Education: Interdistrict Data for Panjab and Haryana (N = 15)

Log Fertiliser/Hec. = Log b_0 + b_1 Log Ed.

Year	Education 1			Education 2			Education 3			Education 4			Education 5			Education 6		
	b co-eff.	T. Value	$\bar{R}^2$	b co-eff.	T. Value	$\bar{R}^2$	b co-eff.	T. Value	$\bar{R}^2$	b co-eff.	T. Value	$\bar{R}^2$	b co-eff.	T. Value	$\bar{R}^2$	b co-eff.	T. Value	$\bar{R}^2$
1961	0.487	0.6	0.125	1.678	4.5	0.550	1.230	6.0	0.697	−0.733	0.8	0.103	1.616	3.0	0.316	1.475	5.9	0.634
1962	1.084	1.1	0.050	2.049	4.5	0.550	1.610	8.6	0.826	−0.187	0.2	0.151	1.883	2.8	0.289	1.817	7.1	0.761
1963	0.567	0.6	0.119	1.815	3.8	0.446	1.514	7.6	0.737	−0.312	0.3	0.144	1.732	2.7	0.263	1.680	6.8	0.748
1964	0.394	0.5	0.135	1.714	3.1	0.344	1.558	7.2	0.771	−0.267	0.3	0.145	1.620	2.4	0.190	1.672	6.4	0.722
1965	0.382	0.4	0.136	1.760	2.7	0.270	1.736	7.6	0.766	−0.130	0.2	0.152	1.722	2.2	0.160	1.839	6.6	0.736
1966	0.436	0.5	0.131	1.787	2.4	0.192	1.892	6.1	0.704	0.039	0.0	0.154	1.808	2.0	0.120	1.966	5.9	0.682
1967	0.349	0.5	0.135	1.324	1.6	0.044	1.668	4.4	0.530	0.097	0.1	0.152	1.382	1.5	0.010	1.706	4.3	0.518
1968	0.447	0.6	0.123	0.910	0.9	0.082	1.701	3.4	0.386	0.280	0.4	0.141	1.030	0.9	0.085	1.770	3.5	0.414
1969	0.390	0.6	0.121	0.541	0.6	0.125	1.474	2.9	0.295	0.280	0.5	0.136	0.676	0.6	0.121	1.545	3.1	0.340
1970	0.399	0.7	0.114	0.206	0.2	0.150	1.407	2.6	0.232	0.322	0.6	0.125	0.344	0.3	0.146	1.498	2.9	0.297
1971	0.367	0.6	0.121	−0.071	0.1	0.153	1.437	2.2	0.163	0.311	0.5	0.129	0.017	0.0	0.154	1.558	2.6	0.236

use of HYV seeds and we have seen that the higher the proportion of cultivators with completed secondary education, the larger is the use of chemical fertiliser per hectare. In fact, rather surprisingly, the elasticity of the coefficient of E_6 is greater than unity for all the years.

The results of equations 3.2 and 3.3 where we examined the relationship between yield per hectare and the use of chemical fertiliser per hectare with education suggest that education of the farm workers is in all probability an important factor in determining the level of agricultural productivity and the use of yield raising inputs like chemical fertilisers. It can be argued that districts with a higher proportion of educated workers might have greater irrigation facilities, greater access to credit, greater ability to bear risks and therefore there is a covariance between productivity per hectare, use of chemical fertilisers per hectare and the proportion of educated farm workers. One can question the causal chain. We shall discuss this problem in chapter 4 where we examine the causal chain and chapter 5 where we examine the farm level production functions. For the moment, we shall assume that our presumption regarding the causal chain is probably right.

We examine the stability of the structural relation presented in equations 3.2 and 3.3 during the period 1961 to 1972 using the 'Chow' test for stability of coefficients.[8] The results of the Chow tests with yield per hectare as the dependent variable are reported in Appendix Table A.1, and for fertiliser use per hectare as the dependent variable in Appendix Table A.2. The estimated F Values with E_2, E_3 and E_6 for yield per hectare as well as for fertiliser used per hectare indicates that the coefficients over the period have changed significantly. This means that the structural relation has not remained stable during 1961 to 1972.

Having obtained the result that the slope of the relationship between yield per hectare and education has significantly changed over the period 1961 to 1972 for districts of Panjab and Haryana, we attempted to measure the change of slope by using a slope dummy.[9] We postulated a relationship of the following type:

$$\text{Y/Hec } 1961 = a_1 + b_1 x_1 \tag{3.4}$$

$$\text{Y/Hec } 1971 = a_2 + b_2 x_2 \tag{3.5}$$

$$\text{Y/Hec } (1961 + 1971) = (a_1 + a_2) + b_1 (x_1 + x_2)$$
$$+ \frac{b_2 x_2 - b_1 x_1}{(b_2 - b_1) x} \tag{3.6}$$

We can rewrite this as,

$$Y = a + bx + (b - c) \, WX \qquad\qquad (3.7)$$

where WX is the dummy to measure the change of slope between 1961 and 1972.

The statistical coefficients for relationships measured in 1961 and 1972 separately and with slope dummies are given in table 3.8.

The change of slope for 1961 to 1972 is positive and is of the order of +0.662 for the secondary education of the cultivators explaining yield per hectare. Our measure of the change of the slope is in effect a statistical measure of the 'innovative effect' of education in this region. If the slope had remained unchanged during this period of the Green Revolution, we could have argued that the positive relationship between education and yield per hectare was because both are positively related to some other factor and the correlation between the two may be spurious. The causation hypothesised by us in such a situation would have been inappropriate. If the slope had been negatively affected by the Green Revolution we could have argued that the relationship between education and yield per hectare as postulated by us was essentially representing a wrong causation because in such a situation it would be higher productivity which would enable the cultivators to acquire education and thus education would be the result of higher yield rather than the cause of it. A change of slope of the order of +0.662 for secondary education of cultivators and yield per hectare clearly suggests that the relationship between education and yield per hectare over the eleven year period has become stronger. This, in all probability, is because the direction of the causation suggested in the present study is right and a measure of the change of slope is largely a measure of the 'innovative effect' of education.

Of the six alternative measures of education originally proposed we dropped E_1 and E_4, viz., the proportion of literate farm workers and the proportion of literate cultivators, as not relevant for explaining productivity or fertiliser use. Of the remaining four measures (E_2, E_3, E_5, E_6) the largest numerical value is for E_6 (secondary education among cultivators). This clearly suggests that the level of education which explains productivity or fertiliser use is secondary education among cultivators in Panjab and Haryana.

We applied the 'Chow' test to the relationship between yield and fertiliser use per hectare and education for the four years 1968-9 to 1971-2. The results are reported in Appendix Table A.3 and A.4. These results indicate that the structural relationships during this period have not changed. This enabled us to pool 4 years' time series data for a

Table 3.8: Interdistrict Data — Change of Slope, 1961–1972

Education level		Means		Period (1961 + 1972) with Dummies				Change of Slope $(b_1 - c_1)\frac{\bar{X}_2}{\bar{X}_1}$	Value of $b_2 = b_1 + (b_1 - c_1)\frac{\bar{X}_2}{\bar{X}_1}$ Slope in 1972
		1961 $(\bar{X}_1)$	1972 $(\bar{X}_2)$	b_1 slope in 1961	c_1	$(b_1 - c_1)$	$\frac{\bar{X}_2}{\bar{X}_1}$		
Yield/Hec.									
Primary Ed	(E_2)	-1.097	-0.791	0.423	-0.565	0.988	0.721	0.712	1.135
Secondary Ed	(E_3)	-1.890	-1.489	0.486	-0.248	0.734	0.788	0.578	1.064
Primary Ed of Cultivators only	(E_5)	-0.982	-0.720	0.447	-0.634	1.081	0.733	0.792	1.239
Secondary Ed of Cultivators only	(E_6)	-1.747	-1.370	0.596	-0.248	0.844	0.784	0.662	1.258
Fertiliser/Hec.									
Primary Ed	(E_2)			1.459	-1.189	2.648		1.909	3.368
Secondary Ed	(E_3)			1.481	-0.513	1.994		1.571	3.052
Primary Ed of Cultivators only	(E_5)			1.525	-1.361	2.886		2.115	3.640
Secondary Ed of Cultivators only	(E_6)			1.744	-0.514	2.258		1.770	3.514

cross section of 15 districts, giving us a total of 60 observations.[10] We estimated the following equation with a view to study the relationship between incidence of secondary education among agricultural workers (E_3), and among cultivators (E_6) and the proportion of area under HYV seeds:

$$\text{Log } Y = \log b_0 + b_1 \log \text{Education} \qquad (3.8)$$

where   Y = Proportion of area under HYV seeds
         E = Incidence of education $[(E_3) \text{ and } E_6)]$[11]

The estimated elasticity coefficients are given below:

Table 3.9: Relationship between Education and Adoption of HYV Seed Interdistrict Data for Panjab and Haryana, 1968–72

	Variables	(N = 60) Co-eff.	(Variables in Logs) T. Values	$\bar{R}^2$
1.	Education$_3$	0.884	3.294	0.129
2.	Education$_6$	0.936	3.623	0.156

As expected the coefficients with E_3 and E_6 are both statistically significant at the 1 per cent level. The value of $\bar{R}^2$ and the numerical value of the elasticity coefficient are somewhat higher with E_6 which should be expected because decision to use HYV seed lies with the cultivators only. Therefore, the relevant measure of education is the incidence of secondary education among cultivators (E_6).

In Panjab and Haryana states, use of co-operative facilities for agricultural credit has been growing rapidly; co-operative credit societies have been in existence in these areas for a long time. We postulated the following relationship to check if membership of co-operative societies (Y) is related to incidence of education among cultivators (E_6):

$$\text{Log } Y = \log b_0 + b_1 \log E_6 \qquad (3.9)$$

The estimated co-efficients are reported in Table 3.10.

The elasticity coefficient of E_6 is statistically significant at the 1 per cent level suggesting that incidence of secondary education among cultivators has a positive impact on the growth of co-operative facilities measured in terms of membership.

Table 3.10: Relationship between Education and Membership of Co-operative Societies: Interdistrict Data for Panjab and Haryana 1968–1972

	Variables	(N = 60) Co-eff.	(Variables in Logs) T. Value	$\bar{R}^2$
1.	Constant	2.699	17.610	0.092
2.	Education$_6$	0.303	2.840	

Absence of a statistically significant relationship between literacy and productivity and the use of modernising inputs like fertilisers suggests two possibilities. Either literacy has a largely social value or the benefits of literacy have become so diffused that these have taken the form of an externality which we have not been able to capture statistically. Chaudhri (1968) examining the evidence from this region for 1961 argued that it is the problem of measuring an externality that has led to the observed statistical results.

The relationship between elementary education and productivity and the use of chemical fertilisers was positive and significant for the pre-Green Revolution period (1961 to 1966) but statistically not significant after 1967. This probably suggests that the level of education relevant for the diffusion of innovations depends on the degree of sophistication of the innovations being considered. This finding, if correct, has interesting implications for educational policy.

In the statistical exercises reported in this chapter we observed a positive and statistically significant relationship between secondary education among cultivators (E_6) and farm workers (E_3), and agricultural productivity per hectare, use of chemical fertilisers per hectare, area under high yielding varieties of seed and institutional facilities like co-operatives. These results create a strong presumption that secondary education among cultivators, if our hypothesising of direction of causation is right, has facilitated the diffusion of innovations leading to the Green Revolution in this area. We shall examine the direction of causation in the next chapter.

Notes

1. Some of the details about growth of tractorisations are reported in a study

by Panjab Agricultural University, *The Dynamics of Panjab Agriculture* (Ludhiana 1972).

2. Shakuntala Mehra (1966) attempted to estimate surplus labour in different states of India by using estimates of labour demand based on the Farm Management Studies for 1955–57. Her study suggested a surplus of agricultural labour in Panjab. This finding conflicts with K. N. Raj's assertion in his book *Economics of Bhakra Nangal Project* (Asia Publishing House, Bombay, 1959), that even during the early 1950s labour was not available from within Panjab for work on Bhakra Nangal dam and its irrigation systems. Therefore, the Bhakra Nangal Project authorities had to import labour from the neighbouring states of Rajasthan and UP. Our objective is not to examine the question of the existence of surplus labour but to examine whether education can lead to its more effective use through higher productivity.

3. We have data on 15 districts. When we include 7 explanatory variables, we are left with 7 degrees of freedom. This partly explains why many of the coefficients are statistically not significant. Multicollinearity among variables is also very high as reported in Table 3.2.

4. One can argue that growth of education is the result rather than the cause of growth of output. We shall determine the causal chain in Chapter 4 and discuss this point in detail there.

5. We are hypothesising that it is education, and factors having direct and high correlation with education, which is causing variation in yield per hectare.

6. Note that the regression equations are linear in logs. Therefore, the estimated b coefficients are elasticities.

7. The relationship between the proportion of area under HYV seed and education is itself very strong. These results are reported in subsequent sections.

8. For details regarding the application of 'Chow' test, see Rao and Miller (1970), Kuh (1971) and D. Haung (1971).

9. For justification of this procedure see Rao and Miller (1970).

10. For statistical aspects of pooling of time series and cross section data, see Klein (1964), Kuh (1971).

11. We estimated this equation with E_3 and E_6 only because the results reported in earlier sections of this chapter (see tables 3.6 and 3.7) indicated that after 1966-7 it is E_3 and E_6 that have statistically significant relationships with yield and fertiliser use.

4 DETERMINING THE CAUSAL CHAIN

The statistical relationships explored in chapter 3 are all based on the causal chain that we have hypothesised — that it is the general education of cultivators and farm workers which influences the use of chemical fertilisers, the area under HYV seeds and the value of output per hectare. But it is reasonable to argue that the causation could also be the other way around i.e., the greater ability to pay for education which comes from a higher yield per hectare and a larger use of chemical fertiliser per hectare, enables cultivating households in this region to send their children to school; with a lag, they join the labour force and are regarded as farmers with general education. It is essential to explore firstly what are the variables which move together and secondly, the statistical possibilities that the causal chain could be different from what we have hypothesised in the last chapter. This is reported in this chapter.

The Inter-relatedness of Education and other Variables

The zero order correlations of various input factors, agricultural output and three alternative measures of education based on inter-district data for the years 1968-9 to 1971-2[1] are reported in table 4.1. We find that net area sown, area sown more than once, number of tractors in the district, number of tubewells in the district, use of fertiliser per hectare and value of agricultural produce per hectare and the incidence of education E_3 (secondary education among all farm workers) and E_6 (secondary education among cultivators) have a high positive correlation. The actual magnitudes of the correlation coefficients vary between +.45 and +.92. Correlation coefficients of this order are statistically significant and cannot be observed by chance association only.

To explore the degree of inter-relatedness of all these variables with factors independently of each other we used factor analysis. The main variable clusters based on factor score coefficients and factor loadings with a rotated varimax factor analysis are reported in table 4.2. We find that the first factor explains a variance of 43.4 per cent, the second factor explains a variance of 25.0 per cent while the third and subsequent factors individually explain 10 per cent or less of the total variance. Therefore, for our purposes the two crucial factors which

Table 4.1: Zero Order Correlation of Interdistrict Pooled Data of Panjab and Haryana: 1968–9 to 1971–2   (N = 60)

(0) Variables	Net Sown Area (1)	Total Labour Force (2)	Tractors (3)	Tube-wells (4)	(E₁) (5)	(E₃) (6)	(E₆) (7)	Area under HYV/NSA (8)	Yield/Hec. (9)	Fertiliser/Hectare (10)	Intensity of Cropping (11)	Agr. Lab./Total Labour Force (12)	Agr. Wages (Ploughing) (13)
1. Net Sown Area		0.913	0.548	0.104	0.148	−0.580	−0.377	−0.360	−0.360	−0.489	−0.335	−0.009	0.272
2. Total Labour Force			0.688	0.320	0.198	−0.515	−0.449	−0.149	−0.086	−0.270	−0.102	0.243	0.285
3. Tractors				0.463	0.272	−0.130	−0.036	0.186	0.217	0.092	0.044	0.468	0.362
4. Tubewells					0.098	0.152	0.218	0.530	0.596	0.460	0.511	0.388	0.389
5. (E_1)						−0.039	0.042	0.243	0.269	0.259	0.239	0.336	−0.083
6. (E_3)							0.987	0.612	0.580	0.685	0.414	0.277	0.092
7. (E_6)								0.681	0.659	0.750	0.467	0.394	0.114
8. Area under HYV/NSA									0.916	0.925	0.599	0.611	0.306
9. Yield/Hectare										0.901	0.710	0.698	0.185
10. Fertiliser/Hectare											0.631	0.636	0.116
11. Intensity of Cropping												0.568	−0.010
12. Agr. Labour/Total Labour Force													−0.010
13. Agr. Wages (Ploughing)													

Table 4.2: Main Variable Clusters based on Factor Score Coefficients from Factor Analysis and Rotated Varimax Factor Analysis
(Interdistrict Pooled Data – Time Series and Cross Section)   (N = 60)

Variables	Factors			Rotated Factors		
	F_1	F_2	F_3	F_1	F_2	F_3
	(1)	(2)	(3)	(4)	(5)	(6)
1. Net Sown Area	0.526	0.782	-0.040	0.244	0.871	-0.153
2. Total Labour Force	0.283	0.908	0.009	0.040	0.900	-0.112
3. Tractors	-0.118	0.842	-0.070	-0.125	0.488	-0.171
4. Tubewells	-0.520	0.556	-0.242	-0.357	0.185	-0.193
5. Ed_1/Total Labour Force	-0.780	0.388	-0.233	-0.310	-0.299	-0.051
7. Ed_6/Total Labour Force	-0.780	-0.388	-0.233	-0.310	-0.298	-0.051
8. HYV Area/NSA	-0.921	0.139	-0.082	-0.864	-0.120	-0.197
9. Yield/Hectare	-0.934	0.189	0.046	-0.813	-0.073	-0.063
10. Fert./Hectare	-0.950	0.005	0.052	-0.816	-0.203	-0.025
11. Intensity of Cropping	-0.740	0.100	0.242	-0.397	-0.098	0.045
12. Agr. Labourers/ Total Lab. Force	-0.659	0.442	0.349	-0.544	0.197	0.114
13. Agr. Wages (Ploughing)	-0.155	0.429	-0.759	-0.121	0.188	-0.953
% Variance explained by factors	43.4	25.0	10.1			
Cumulative % Variance explained by Factors	43.4	68.4	78.5			

need looking at are factor 1 and factor 2 which between them explain about 68 per cent of total variations.

The first factor is very strongly *but negatively* related with the proportion of cultivators with secondary education (factor score −0.84), tractors (factor loading −0.12), value of produce per hectare (factor loading −0.93), fertiliser use per hectare (factor loading −0.95), intensity of cropping (factor loading −0.74) and number of tubewells (factor loading −0.52). Interestingly enough only two variables, included in the factor analysis, namely net sown area and total agricultural labour force, have a positive factor loading in the case of the first factor with a score of 0.52 and 0.28 respectively. The second factor has a positive factor loading with net sown area (0.78), intensity of cropping (0.10), number of agricultural workers (0.91), tractors (0.84) and tubewell (0.56). This suggests that the first factor seems to be common to all the variables included in the analysis except area sown and there is a strong inter-relatedness between fertiliser use, tractors, tubewells, intensity of cropping (area sown more than once), proportion of farm workers with secondary education and incidence of secondary education among cultivators. The second factor operates positively with net area sown, intensity of cropping, tubewells, value of agricultural produce per hectare and fertiliser use per hectare.

Factor loading, when rotated with rotated varimax technique, indicates that the first factor is negatively related with the value of agricultural produce per hectare (−0.81), the proportion of cultivators with secondary education (−0.38), the proportion of agricultural workers with secondary education (−0.31), the number of tubewells in the district (−0.36) and the number of tractors in the district (−0.13). The second factor in rotated factor loading has a strong positive value with net sown area (+0.87), the agricultural labour force (+0.90) and a negative value with the proportion of cultivators with secondary education (−0.25) and the value of agricultural produce per hectare (−0.07). These factor loadings suggest that rotated varimax factor loading has not changed the pattern significantly and the negative relationships of the first factor with the variables mentioned above and the positive factor loading with the variables mentioned above shows a more or less similar pattern. This further underlines the fact of inter-relatedness of factors which are conventionally considered as yield raising modern input factors and the general educational level of the cultivators and agricultural workers.

Determining the Causal Chain

In chapter 2 we had hypothesised that in all probability the educational
level of the cultivator influences his choice of yield raising inputs like
the use of high yielding variety seeds and chemical fertilisers which
influence the gross value of agricultural produce. It is also possible that
the gross value of agricultural produce influences the level of education
of the cultivators through its influence on farming families' abilities to
pay for this education. To take account of simultaneity in demand for
education, use of chemical fertilisers and value of agricultural produce
and their mutual interdependence we set up a simultaneous equation
system with the following specifications:

$$Y_1 = f(Y_2, Y_3, X_1, X_2, X_3) \qquad (4.1)$$
$$Y_2 = f(Y_1, Y_3, X_4, X_5) \qquad (4.2)$$
$$Y_3 = f(Y_1, X_6) \qquad (4.3)$$

where,

Y_1 = Gross value of agricultural produce
Y_2 = Chemical Fertilisers used
Y_3 = Secondary education among cultivators (E_6)
X_1 = Total cropped area (Hectares)
X_2 = Number of cultivators
X_3 = Number of agricultural labourers
X_4 = Proportion of total cropped area under HYV seed
X_5 = Number of tubewells
X_6 = Enrolment ratios in secondary schools

In this simultaneous equation system gross value of agricultural
produce (Y_1), use of chemical fertilisers (Y_2) and secondary education
among cultivators (Y_3), are the three endogenous variables, and total
cropped area (X_1), number of cultivators (X_2), number of agricultural
labourers (X_3), proportion of area under HYV seed (X_4), number of
tubewells (X_5) and enrolment ratios in secondary classes (X_6) are the
six exogenous variables.

It is reasonable to expect that the gross value of agricultural produce
would depend upon the use of the chemical fertilisers, total cropped
area, number of cultivators, number of agricultural labourers and the
incidence of secondary education among cultivators. These appear as
explanatory variables in the first equation.

Use of chemical fertilisers might be influenced by farming families'
abilities to pay for the purchase of fertilisers which would be influenced

by the gross value of agricultural produce. Use of chemical fertilisers might also be influenced by the incidence of secondary education among cultivators reflecting their superior information field which can be translated into practice by a larger use of fertilisers. The HYV seeds can be used only in a package with proper doses of fertilisers and an assured irrigation supply. Therefore, in the second equation we use gross value of agricultural produce, incidence of education among cultivators, proportion of area under HYV and number of tubewells as the explanatory variables.

It is possible that the incidence of secondary education among cultivators would depend upon the gross value of agricultural produce indicating farming families' abilities to pay for education and would represent the demand for education while enrolment ratios in secondary classes would be a surrogate for the supply of education. We expect that the gross value of agricultural produce (i.e., demand for education) and the enrolment ratios in secondary classes (i.e., supply of education), would both have positive slopes. Separating demand from supply will be statistically difficult and in any case is not necessary for our purpose. With the simultaneous equation system we are, in essence, examining whether the influence of secondary education among cultivators, on the use of chemical fertilisers and value of agricultural produce, as hypothesised in the earlier chapters of the study, is real or a statistical illusion.

To estimate this simultaneous equation system we use data from fifteen districts from Panjab and Haryana for the four years 1968-9 to 1971-2. Before pooling time series and cross section data we tested for the stability of the structural relationship during the period 1968-9 to 1971-2 using the Chow test and found that the structural relationship has not changed during these years (see Appendix Tables A.3 and A.4). Pooling of time series and cross section data for these four years gave us a total of sixty observations. The proposed simultaneous equations model, as may be noted, is over-identified. It has therefore been estimated by two stage least square (TSLS) procedure. Log linear functional forms are assumed for all the three equations and the model is estimated using interdistrict pooled data for 1968-9 to 1971-2. The estimates of the parameters are reported in table 4.3. All the three equations appear to be well estimated in terms of the goodness of fit criterion as well as the Durbin-Watson statistics.

The estimated model conforms well to our expectations. The estimated coefficients of all the exogenous variables included in the equations system are statistically significant at the 1 per cent level.

Table 4.3: Two Stage Least Square Estimates of the Model for Education and Productivity in Panjab and Haryana — 1968-9 to 1971-2   (N = 60)   (Variable in Logs)

Identification	Equations	$\bar{R}^2$	DW	Standard Error of Estimates
Productivity Equation	$Y_1 = 3.079 + 0.274$ (Fertilisers) $+ 0.960$ (Education of Cult) (0.066) (0.276) $+ 1.327$ (Total Cropped Area) $- 0.646$ (Cultivators) (0.195) (0.248) $- 0.528$ (Agr. Labourer) (0.196)	0.939	1.514	0.163
Fertilisers	$Y_2 = 2.375 - 1.170$ (Productivity) $+ 2.040$ (Education of Cult) (0.212) (0.329) $+ 0.968$ (HYV) $- 0.065$ (Tubewells) (0.140) (0.102)	0.835	1.203	0.363
Education of Cultivators	$Y_3 = 2.527 + 0.389$ (Productivity) $+ 0.288$ (Students in (0.079) (0.100) Classes IX—XI)	0.609	1.311	0.239

Note: Figures in parenthesis are the standard errors of the corresponding estimates.

The productivity equation has an $\bar{R}^2$ of 0.94. The influence of two endogenous variables, namely, fertilisers and the incidence of secondary education among cultivators, is significant at the 1 per cent level with elasticity coefficient of 0.27 in case of fertilisers and 0.96 in case of education of the cultivators. The elasticity coefficient for the exogenous variable of total cropped area is also significant at the 1 per cent level with elasticity of 1.33. The contribution of cultivators and agricultural labourers has a negative sign. This is very surprising. But our definition of cultivators and labourers is in terms of number of persons reported to be working in this area in the sense of persons deriving their livelihood from agriculture. We have no indication about the degree of unemployment, under-employment or disguised unemployment among cultivators or incidence of open unemployment among agricultural labourers. Therefore, the negative coefficients for the agricultural labour force are probably because the variables are poorly measured. The possibility of substitution between labour and chemical fertilisers is also not completely ruled out.

The second equation for fertiliser use has a negative coefficient for the value of agricultural produce, with an elasticity of -1.2. This is somewhat surprising. We know that there has been considerable expansion in co-operative credit in this area. A large number of state sponsored programmes to help small farmers, like the Small Farmers Development Agency (a part of Special Employment Programme), have been in operation and these induced smaller cultivators to use HYV seeds and fertilisers. These are offered on credit at reasonable rates of interest (8 to 9 per cent per annum). Therefore, this negative but statistically insignificant coefficient indicates that in all probability the use of chemical fertilisers, which in the initial stages looks risky, is undertaken only when institutional credit with a reasonably low interest rate is available. The coefficient of the incidence of secondary education among cultivators is significant at the 1 per cent level with an elasticity of 2.04 and that of the proportion of the area under HYV is also significant at the 1 per cent level with an elasticity of 0.97. The coefficient for tubewells is statistically insignificant probably because there is a high degree of inter-relatedness between the number of tubewells and the proportion of HYV and tubewells (simple correlation between these two variables is of the order of .79; see Appendix Table A.5).

For the third equation (for education) the value of $\bar{R}^2$ is 0.61. Both the coefficients of the value of agricultural produce and the enrolment ratios in secondary classes are significant at the 1 per cent level with elasticity coefficients of 0.39 and 0.29 respectively. This suggests that farmers' abilities to pay and states' effort to expand secondary education both influence the incidence of secondary education among cultivators.

An interesting point worth noting is that even when education is an endogenous variable, its contribution to the use of chemical fertilisers is statistically significant at the 1 per cent level with a remarkably high elasticity coefficient of 2.04. Even when the use of fertiliser itself is an endogenous variable and is included in the value of agricultural produce, the coefficient of education remains statistically significant at the 1 per cent level with an elasticity of 0.96. This suggests once again that the influence of a cultivator's education is not only on his choice of inputs like chemical fertilisers but also on various other things which influence the value of agricultural produce like crop husbandry practices, the combination of optimal proportions of inputs, choice of right crop-mix etc. These results are highly suggestive of the fact that the causal chain we had hypothesised in the earlier chapters is right and education is a relevant factor in agricultural production and the diffusion of innovations.

We tested the stability of these coefficients by changing the value of the exogenous variables by one unit in each case and computing multipliers of endogenous variables with respect to exogenous variables called elacticity multipliers. The coefficients in all cases turn out to be stable and the value of elasticity multipliers of endogenous variables with respect to exogenous variables are reported in table 4.4.

The reduced form of elasticity multipliers measures the total response of endogenous variables for percentage change in the exogenous variable. For example, one per cent rise in the gross cropped area causes 1.82 per cent increase in the gross value of agricultural produce (GAP). These results are in the expected direction.

Thus we find that in the simultaneous equations system when incidence of education among cultivators (E_6) is an endogenous variable, its positive relationship with use of chemical fertilisers, area under HYV seed and the gross value of agricultural produce remains significant, suggesting that the hypothesised causal chain is, in all probability, correct.

Note

1. Statistical results of 'Chow' test discussed in Chapter 3 indicated that the structural relationship between 1961–72 has not remained stable but for the period 1968–72 it has been stable. Therefore we pooled 4 years' data for 15 districts.

Table 4.4: Simultaneous Equations Model: The Reduced Form Elasticity Multipliers of Endogenous Variables with Respect to Exogenous Variables
Interdistricts' Pooled Data for Panjab and Haryana: 1968-9 to 1971-2   (N = 60)

	Exogenous Variables					
	Total Cropped Area [449.8]	Cultivators [161100.0]	Agricultural Labour [61940.0]	Area under HYV [116.4]	Tube-wells [7031.0]	No. of Students [19770.0]
1. Gross Value of Agricultural Produce [5152.0]	1.819 (2.546)	−0.886 (−0.632)	−0.724 (−0.560)	0.363 (0.652)	−0.024 (−0.023)	0.221 (0.191)
2. Fertiliser [12110.0]	0.685 (1.054)	−0.333 (−0.261)	−0.272 (−0.232)	0.831 (1.642)	−0.056 (−0.059)	0.600 (0.570)
3. Education$_6$ [6039.0]	0.704 (1.003)	−0.344 (−0.250)	−0.281 (−0.222)	0.141 (0.258)	−0.009 (−0.009)	0.316 (0.278)

Note: Figures in square brackets are geometric means; figures in parentheses are marginal products.

5 EDUCATION, ENTREPRENEURSHIP AND FARM BUSINESS

In this chapter we attempt a statistical estimate of the worker effect of a cultivator's education, if any, with the help of interhousehold data pertaining to 1038 cultivating households in the wheat belt of north India. These households are from 19 villages of Panjab, Haryana and UP for one agricultural year during the early 1960s.[1] All these villages are from the wheat belt of north India and have characteristics very similar to those of the districts analysed in the preceding chapters.

We begin the statistical analysis of these household data by estimating the parameters of an unrestricted Cobb-Douglas production function with the following specifications:

$$Y = AX_1^{b_1} X_2^{b_2} X_3^{b_3} X_4^{b_4} X_5^{b_5} X_6^{b_6} X_7^{b_7} \qquad (5.1)$$

where,

Y = Gross Value of Agricultural Produce (Rupees)
X_1 = Area Cultivated Unirrigated (Acres)
X_2 = Area Cultivated Irrigated (Acres)
X_3 = Value of Seeds (Rupees)
X_4 = Value of Chemical Fertiliser (Rupees)
X_5 = Value of Farm Yard Manure (FYM)
X_6 = Value of Labour used (Rupees)
X_7 = Number of Bullocks

The estimating equation, linear in logs is:

$$\log Y = \log A + b_1 \log x_1 + b_2 \log x_2 + b_3 \log x_3 + b_4 \log x_4 \\ + b_5 \log x_5 + b_6 \log x_6 + b_7 \log x_7 \qquad (5.2)$$

The zero order correlation among different variables is reported in table 5.1. Multicollinearity does not seem to be a problem with this set of data. The correlation matrix supports many of the familiar conjectures about the agriculture of this region for the early sixties, like joint use of farm yard manure (FYM) and fertilisers, complementarity between labour cost, and fertiliser use, and irrigation and fertiliser use, etc.

The estimates of the parameters are reported in table 5.2. All the coefficients with the above specification are well estimated and are

51

Table 5.1: Zero Order Correlation of Selected Variables   (Household Data for Panjab and UP for early 1960s)
(N = 1038)

Variables (a)	Cultivated area (1)	Irrigated (2)	Agriculture (3)	Seeds (4)	Fertilisers (5)	FYM (6)	Labour Cost (7)	Milch Cattle (8)	Bullocks (9)	Years of Schooling of the HH Head (10)	Years of Schooling of Agr. Workers in HH (11)
Cult. Area		.009	.310	.139	.088	.149	.054	.290	−.041	.188	.192
Irrig. Area			.571	.511	.170	.388	.383	.506	−.165	.129	.245
Ag. Produce				.497	.416	.399	.447	.815	−.096	.265	.372
Seeds					.248	.348	.270	.453	−.166	.172	.218
Fertilisers						.226	.282	.250	.066	.137	.133
FYM							.288	.289	.020	.090	.156
Lab. Cost								.371	−.050	.146	.345
Milch Cattle									−.144	.206	.332
Bullocks										−.184	−.200
Yrs. of Schooling of Head of HH											.648
Yrs. of Schooling of Agr. Workers in HH											

Table 5.2: Parameters of Cobb-Douglas Production Function with the Education of Agricultural Workers in the Household (N = 1038) (Household Data for Panjab and UP for early 1960s)

Variable Name (a)	Without Dummies and with Education		With Income Dummies		With Caste Dummies		Without Education and without Dummies	
	Co-eff. (1)	t-Value (2)	Co-eff. (3)	t-Value (4)	Co-eff. (5)	t-Value (6)	Co-eff. (7)	t-Value (8)
Constant	2.216	22.931	-1.254	-0.001	-0.941	-0.001	2.103	22.111
1. Cultivated Area	0.222	9.978	0.116	6.267	0.221	9.267	0.236	10.579
2. Irrigated Area	0.308	12.046	0.156	7.192	0.307	11.419	0.317	12.253
3. Seeds	0.058	4.956	0.014	1.503	0.058	4.730	0.060	5.159
4. Fertilisers	0.129	13.635	0.094	11.864	0.128	12.848	0.132	13.767
5. FYM	0.024	2.036	0.032	3.386	0.023	1.888	0.022	1.863
6. Labour	0.182	5.178	0.089	3.065	0.182	4.962	0.226	6.571
7. Cattle	0.030	2.946	0.009	1.121	0.029	2.687	0.033	3.206
8. Years of Schooling of Agr. Workers in the HH	0.116	5.043	0.051	2.699	0.119	4.852		
9. Income Group I			3.753	0.004				
10. Income Group II			4.113	0.004				
11. Income Group III			4.260	0.004				
12. Income Group IV			4.446	0.004				
13. Caste I					3.142	0.003		
14. Caste II					3.152	0.003		
15. Caste III					3.160	0.003		
$\bar{R}^2$	0.593		0.730		0.556		0.583	
F Value of the Equation	190.455		234.962		119.092		209.071	

statistically significant at the 1 per cent level, except FYM which is
significant at the 5 per cent level. The coefficient of multiple determination corrected for degrees of freedom ($\bar{R}^2$) is 0.583, and the
equation is well estimated with a F-value of 209. We tested for the
deviation of the sum of the coefficients from unity for return to scale
and found that the sum comes to 1.026 and is not significantly
different from unity in the usual t-test.

To examine the contribution of education, if any, we estimated the
parameters using all the variables included in the foregoing specifications
but added as a measure of education the years of schooling of all the
agricultural workers in the household. This gives us a new specification
of the following type:

$$\text{Log } Y = a + b_1 \log X_1 + b_2 \log X_2 + b_3 \log X_3 + b_4 \log X_4$$
$$+ b_5 \log X_5 + b_6 \log X_6 + b_7 \log X_7 + b_8 \log E \qquad (5.3)$$

We define education in two alternative ways: (a) the number of
years of schooling for all the agricultural workers in the family, and (b)
the years of schooling of the head of the household.[2]

The estimated equation 5.3 is statistically significant: all the
coefficients are well estimated and are significant at the 1 per cent level
of significance. The parameters are reported in table 5.2. All the
earlier coefficients remained stable and the coefficients of education
came to be 0.116 with a standard error of 0.023. The value of the
multiple coefficient of determination ($\bar{R}^2$) increased to 0.593, thus
suggesting that the education of the agricultural workers in the household seems to be a significant factor in production. We decided to
explore the relevant definition of education by specifying this
production relation with all the conventional input factors but changing the definition of education to years of schooling of the head of the
agricultural household. This was done to see if the education of the
head of the household, who is usually the decision maker, has a higher
explanatory value. The estimated parameters with years of schooling
of the head of the household are reported in table 5.3. The education
coefficient is 0.114 with a standard error of 0.031, and is significant
at the 1 per cent level. The equation is well estimated with all the
explanatory variables being significant at the 1 per cent level of
significance. The value of $\bar{R}^2$ after introducing education variables
increased from 0.584 to 0.589. This suggests that our reasoning of
chapter 2 is probably right, namely, that when we specify a production
function with the conventional input factors and include education
as one of the explanatory variables at the farm level, the coefficient of

Table 5.3: Parameters of Cobb-Douglas Production Function with the Education of Household Head
(N=1038) (Household Data for Panjab and UP for early 1960s)

Variable Name (a)	Without Dummies and with Education Co-eff. (1)	t-Value (2)	With Income Dummies Co-eff. (3)	t-Value (4)	With Caste Dummies Co-eff. (5)	t-Value (6)	Without Education and without Dummies Co-eff. (7)	t-Value (8)
Constant	2.125	22.427	−0.629	−0.001	−1.875	−0.002	2.103	22.111
1. Cultivated Area	0.224	10.001	0.114	7.350	0.223	9.095	0.236	10.579
2. Irrigated Area	0.314	12.221	0.157	8.678	0.314	11.450	0.317	12.253
3. Seeds	0.057	4.919	0.014	1.685	0.058	4.032	0.060	5.159
4. Fertilisers	0.128	13.364	0.092	13.929	0.127	12.385	0.132	13.767
5. FYM	0.023	1.996	0.032	4.084	0.023	1.836	0.022	1.863
6. Labour	0.218	6.362	0.102	4.333	0.219	6.000	0.226	6.571
7. Cattle	0.032	3.129	0.010	1.423	0.081	2.804	0.033	3.206
8. Years of Schooling of Head in the Household	0.114	3.647	0.073	3.454	0.110	3.423		
9. Income Group I			3.099	0.003				
10. Income Group II			3.463	0.004				
11. Income Group III			3.612	0.004				
12. Income Group IV			3.796	0.004				
13. Caste I					3.989	0.003		
14. Caste II					3.999	0.003		
15. Caste III					3.999	0.003		
$\bar{R}^2$	0.589		0.812		0.536		0.584	
F Value of the Equation	186.784		375.502		109.917		209.071	

education mainly represents the 'worker effect' of education. This is because the allocative effect and the innovative effect would get reflected in the coefficient of the input factors that are used and which might have been chosen initially because of education (for example the use of chemical fertilisers or high yielding variety seeds). The allocative effect would also get reflected in the higher marginal productivities of the different input factors including farm labour. Thus the coefficient of education which largely represents the worker effect of education is nearly the same whether we define education as years of schooling of all the agricultural workers in the farm household or in terms of years of schooling of the head of the agricultural household. Numerically the coefficient for the former has a higher value (0.116 as against 0.114). In a student's t-test the two values are not significantly different from each other.

It is usually alleged[3] that caste factors significantly alter the educational impact in traditional societies like the Indian rural societies. We tested this hypothesis by dividing these households into three caste groups: higher castes which included Brahmins, Chhatris and other trading classes; cultivating castes which included Rajputs, Jats and other castes whose traditional occupation was cultivation. All other castes which did not belong to these two categories were treated in the third category, namely the lower castes. We introduced dummy variables to take into account the effect, if any, of the caste and estimated the parameters of the production functions with the two alternative definitions of education reported in table 5.2 for years of schooling of the agricultural workers in the household and table 5.3 for years of schooling of the head of the household. The caste dummies are not statistically significant. The coefficients are not altered in any significant way but the value of $\overline{R}^2$ drops to 0.556 implying that in all probability caste factors do not alter the underlying production function.

There is a wide belief that the level of the prosperity of the farming households might considerably influence its production function. Moreover, our hypothesis that it is the education which influences productivity as a causal link rather than the other way round can be questioned if we do not allow for differences in the level of prosperity of the farming households. To take into account these differences we divided the farming households in four income categories:[4] (i) Households with a residual annual income of Rs. 1,500 or less; (ii) Households with a residual annual income of Rs. 1,500 to Rs. 3,000; (iii) Households with a residual annual income of Rs. 3,000 to Rs. 5,000; and

(iv) Households with a residual annual income of more than Rs. 5,000.

We introduced the income factor in the form of dummies and estimated the parameters of the production function reported in table 5.2 with the years of schooling of agricultural workers in the household and in table 5.3 with the years of schooling of the head of the agricultural household. The income dummies turn out to be statistically insignificant. The coefficients are disturbed quite a bit, particularly those of labour, land, education and seeds. The value of $\bar{R}^2$ increases to 0.73. Although the coefficient of education is disturbed, its value still stays positive and also statistically significant at the 1 per cent level.

Thus analysis of the interhousehold data using an unrestricted Cobb-Douglas production function clearly suggests that income differences among households do not significantly shift the production function. The caste differences, as per our definitions of castes, also leave the production function undisturbed. The education variable when introduced in the production function increases the value of $\bar{R}^2$ and the coefficient, no matter how we measure it, stays positive and significant at the 1 per cent level.

Since these household data are from a more or less homogeneous region in terms of climatic conditions and cropping pattern and relates to the early sixties – a period when innovations in agriculture which later came to be known as the Green Revolution had not started – the coefficient of education represents mainly the 'worker effect' of education. The influence of education on choice of inputs (e.g. the use of chemical fertilisers) and the proportions in which the inputs are combined is not reflected in the coefficient of education. This part of educational impact, in the production function, influences the coefficients of various input factors directly. Similarly, the allocation effect of education in terms of better crop practices or timely agricultural operations or accurate decisions regarding crop husbandry would all get reflected in the higher marginal products of other factors like labour, land, irrigation and fertilisers and would not be reflected in the coefficient of education. Therefore, it is reasonable to assume that the coefficient of education in these estimates of the production function is essentially the 'worker effect' of education.

In our two alternative specifications of the education variable, viz., the years of schooling of the agricultural workers in the household and years of schooling of the head of the household, we get similar results. The value of $\bar{R}^2$ increases from 0.584 to 0.593 when we introduce education of agricultural workers in the household and it increases to 0.589 when we introduce education of the head of the household only. The values of the two coefficients are not statistically different from each other. We computed the marginal value products of education and other input variables included in the production function by measuring the inputs and outputs at their 'geometric' mean levels. These are reported in table 5.4. The marginal value product of education of the head of the household is Rs. 153.12 while that of the education of all the workers in the cultivating household is Rs. 107.04. The education of the head of the cultivating household is expected to have a higher marginal value product because it is the head who normally takes entrepreneurial decisions in the cultivating household. The marginal value products (MVP) of other input factors are also in the expected directions.[5]

Notes

1. These data were obtained from the Agricultural Economics Research Centre (AERC), University of Delhi. The AERC collected these data in their Continuous Village Survey Series during 1961–64 by complete enumeration of all the households in these villages, purposively selected. We acquired access to their original household and village schedules. The data for 1038 households pertain to the pre-Green Revolution period. Unfortunately similar data for the post-Green Revolution period at the household level are not available. The Farm Management Studies data do not specify the educational characteristics of the households.

2. For computing years of schooling elementary education has a weight of 4 and secondary education has a weight of 10. These weights are chosen to represent the minimum number of years of schooling required to complete these levels of education.

3. Chaudhri (1968) argued rather forcefully that caste factors are important in altering the influence of education.

4. To take into account the prosperity of farming households it would be wrong to take the gross value of agricultural produce. The correct measure would be net income of the households. With the statistical data we have, we know all about the paid out costs but it is difficult to estimate the cost of home supplied inputs like FYM, labour, entrepreneurial functions and the rental value of the land used. Therefore, the level of prosperity is measured in terms of the gross value of agricultural produce minus all the paid out costs of cultivation. Since technically we cannot call it net income, we have decided to call it 'residual' income. We decided not to measure level of prosperity through the area owned or cultivated because there are large fertility differences in land and the land reform laws make reporting of tenancy (leasing out of land) somewhat unreliable. Therefore, given the statistical data the best measure of the level of prosperity of the household is the 'residual' income. This seems to be appropriate for our purposes in any case because all we are concerned with is to separate out the effect, if any, of the level of prosperity either on the production function or on the educational impact in the production function.

5. For comparison of marginal value products estimated for this region see Saini (1974).

Table 5.4: Elasticities and Marginal Value Products from Farm Level Production Function (N = 1038)
(Household Data for Panjab and UP for early 1960s)

Variables		Geometric Means	Ant. log	$\bar{y}/\bar{x}$	Without Education		With Education 1		With Education 2	
					b co-eff. Elasticity	Marg. Prod.	b co-eff. Elasticity	Marg. Prod.	b co-eff. Elasticity	Marg. Prod.
Gross Value of Agriculture Produce	y	3.259	1816.000							
Cultivated Area	x_1	0.351	2.244	809.27	0.236	190.99	0.224	181.28	0.222	179.66
Irrigated Area	x_2	0.306	2.023	897.68	0.317	284.56	0.314	281.87	0.308	276.49
Seeds	x_3	1.347	22.230	81.69	0.060	4.90	0.057	4.66	0.058	4.74
Fertilisers	x_4	1.049	11.190	162.29	0.132	21.42	0.128	20.77	0.129	20.94
FYM	x_5	1.302	20.040	90.62	0.022	1.99	0.023	2.08	0.024	2.17
Labour	x_6	2.904	301.700	2.27	0.226	0.51	0.218	0.49	0.182	0.41
Cattle	x_7	2.174	149.300	12.16	0.033	0.40	0.032	0.39	0.030	0.36
Education 1	x_8	0.131	1.352	1343.20			0.114	153.12		
Education 2	x_9	0.294	1.968	922.76					0.116	107.00

Education 1: Years of schooling of head in the household.

Education 2: Years of schooling of agricultural workers in the household.

6 AGRICULTURAL WAGES, EMPLOYMENT AND WORKERS' EDUCATION

The census of population provides details on the occupational classifications of the labour force in India. One of the occupational categories is agricultural labourers representing landless agricultural wage labour. The number of agricultural labourers in Panjab and Haryana and their proportion in the agricultural labour force according to the 1961 and 1971 census is given in table 6.1.

Table 6.1: Agricultural Labourers in Panjab and Haryana 1961–71

State	1961 Total Agr. Labour Force	1961 Landless Agr. Labourers	1971 Total Agr. Labour Force	1971 Landless Agr. Labourers	Landless Agr. Labourers as % of total Agr. Labour Force 1961	Landless Agr. Labourers as % of total Agr. Labour Force 1971	Annual Compound Rate of Growth among Landless Agr. Labourers 1961–71
Panjab	1937258	334610	2451858	786705	17.27	32.09	8.9
Haryana	2037150	198654	1732920	430312	9.75	24.83	8.0

A large increase in the proportion of agricultural labourers from 1961 to 1971 is partly because of a change in the definition of cultivators and agricultural labourers between these two censuses and partly because some of the tenants might have been evicted due to the higher profitability of self-cultivation caused by the Green Revolution.[1] These numbers represent the number of persons whose main source of livelihood is agricultural wage labour. What proportion of this is actually employed and for how many days in a year is more relevant for measuring employment.

We have discussed the problem of measurement of magnitude of unemployment in chapter 1. One would expect that the problems of measurement of unemployment among landless agricultural labourers are less serious than those involved in the measurement of unemployment among cultivators. This is not true because most of the agricultural labourers tend to be self-employed also, either on a tiny plot of land leased from someone or in household production, like weaving. In limiting cases, particularly in Panjab and Haryana, cattle rearing is an important source of supplementary income among landless agricultural labourers. Therefore measurement of unemployment in this group is as difficult as among cultivators. However, the available estimates of unemployment among agricultural labourers in Panjab and Haryana are as below:

		Year	Estimated Proportion of Landless Workers Un-employed
(a)	According to estimates of Datar (1961) based on Second Labour Enquiry Committee Report, level of unemployment	1961	4.3%
(b)	According to NSS 25th Round (estimated from table 16.1 for Rural Areas of Panjab and Haryana)	1970–71	3.8%

These figures do not represent the real picture because of the rather strong assumptions in the concepts of employment used. Due to heroic assumptions involved in arriving at these estimates of unemployment it is not very meaningful to comment on changes in employment situation in Panjab agriculture based on these statistical data.

Indirect evidence of employment in agriculture in Panjab and Haryana among agricultural wage earners is more realistic and meaningful. We know from our analysis of the growth of productivity in chapter 3 that output in Panjab and Haryana agriculture grew at an annual rate of over 16 per cent, measured at current prices. This magnitude of growth of output is considerably higher than the rate of growth of the labour force in the agricultural sector in Panjab and Haryana. This has led to large scale immigration (seasonal and quasi permanent) into Panjab and Haryana among agricultural wage earners from the neighbouring states of UP and Rajasthan. There must also have been some substitution between labour and other inputs.

In the absence of any accurate information on the level of employment we analysed statistical data on agricultural wages for agricultural operations like ploughing, with a view to finding out if interdistrict variations in the wage rate can be explained by variations

in the usual factors which are associated with the demand and supply o
agricultural labour in the agricultural sector.[2]

For this purpose we pooled cross section data for 15 districts from
Panjab and Haryana for the four years from 1968-9 to 1971-2. This
pooling is justified in view of the fact that we applied a Chow test to
the results for each of these years separately and to the results from
pooled data to see if the structural relationship between 1968-9 to
1971-2 has remained stable. The results of this Chow test are reported
in Appendix Tables A.3 and A.4 suggesting that the structural relationship has not changed during this period. These fifteen interdistrict
observations for four years give us a total of 60 observations.

The two components that constitute the supply of agricultural
labour are: (i) the number of workers, male and female, who are
reported as cultivators, and (ii) the number of workers, male and femal
who are reported as agricultural labourers in each of these districts.
These data on occupational classification are from the 1961 and 1971
censuses and the figures for the intervening years are interpolated on a
compound growth rate basis. Therefore, the number of persons reporte
to be cultivators and agricultural labourers is the number which derive
their income from work in the agricultural sector. This definition is
more in the nature of number of persons depending on agriculture for
their livelihood rather than input units in a production function. The
nature of this supply curve may be completely flat suggesting that all
of them are willing to work at the current wage rates if they are
labourers and at the current marginal value product for own labour if
they are cultivators. On the other hand the supply curve might be
slowly rising partly because of the disutility of work even among self-
employed persons and partly because inducement for non-participating
females to join the labour force might come only when the wages are
somewhat rising. In any case the supply curve of labour during these
four years is not likely to have shifted significantly. Its slope might
have been horizontal to the X axis or slowly rising.

If we had accurate data on employment, it might have been
interesting to identify demand and supply equations in a simultaneous
equation system. In its absence, we decided to explore the causal
factors affecting interdistrict differences in wage rates using the single
equation system estimated by ordinary least squares. Rao and Miller
(1971, p. 195) pointed out that 'when a researcher obtains a high
$\bar{R}^2$, his result is an estimate either of the supply curve or of the demanc
curve. Which is to be identified from economic theory (accepted values
and signs of parameters) and not from "rules of identification".' We

specify the relationship as follows:

$$\text{Log } Y = \text{Log } a + b_1 \log X_1 + b_2 \log X_2 + b_3 \log X_3 + b_4 \log X_4$$
$$+ b_5 \log X_5 + b_6 \log X_6 \qquad (6.1)$$

where,

Y = Agricultural wage rate measured in terms of kilograms of wheat per day

X_1 = Total Cropped area in the district

X_2 = Proportion of area under HYV

X_3 = Number of cultivators per 1000 acres

X_4 = Number of agricultural labourers per 1000 acres

X_5 = Number of Tractors in the district

X_6 = Proportion of agricultural labourers with completed high school education

We decided to measure agricultural wage rates per day in terms of wheat units rather than in money terms because the relevant wage rate for workers to decide whether to offer their services for employment or not is the real wage and not the nominal wage. Computing an index of real wage is beset with serious difficulties common to all index number constructions.[3] Therefore, we decided to convert the reported money wages into kilograms of wheat equivalent using the price of wheat prevalent during the relevant year.

The zero order correlation between the agricultural wage rate and other variables is reported in table 6.2. We find that wages are positively related to all the factors constituting demand factors like net sown area, area sown more than once (intensity of cropping), number of tractors and area under high yielding varieties of seed. The strongest simple correlation of interdistrict variation of wages is with area under high yielding variety (0.57). The simple correlation between wages and number of cultivators is negative though with a small magnitude (−0.09). We estimated three equations with three alternative specifications: (i) without tractors or education; (ii) with tractors but without education, and finally; (iii) with tractors and with education variables. In all the three cases the equations are well estimated. The estimated coefficients and other statistics are reported in table 6.3.

All the coefficients in the first equation are well estimated and are significant at the 1 per cent level. The value of $\bar{R}^2$ is 0.552 and the signs of the coefficients are in the right direction. Total cropped area and high yielding varieties have positive signs as explanatory variables while the number of cultivators and agricultural labourers have

Table 6.2: Analysis of Interdistrict Differences in Agricultural Wages (Ploughing)
Zero Order Correlation – Interdistrict Data for Panjab and Haryana: 1968–72
(N = 60) (Variables in Logs)

(a)	Net Sown Area (1)	Area Sown more than once (2)	Total Labour (3)	Tractors (4)	Education (E_3) (5)	Education (E_6) (6)	Area under HYV (7)	Total Cultivators (8)	Agr. Wages for Ploughing (9)	Total Cropped Area (10)	Agr. Labourers (11)	Education (E_7) (12)	HYV Proportion (13)
1. Net Sown Area		0.825	0.918	0.584	0.360	0.351	0.427	0.158	0.230	0.980	0.790	−0.045	−0.339
2. Area Sown more than once			0.900	0.629	0.569	0.520	0.571	0.115	0.223	0.919	0.864	0.276	−0.129
3. Total Labour				0.727	0.625	0.583	0.608	0.160	0.226	0.950	0.932	0.289	−0.118
4. Tractors					0.716	0.665	0.800	0.080	0.458	0.625	0.771	0.757	0.373
5. Education (E_3)						0.939	0.697	0.097	0.333	0.448	0.683	0.547	0.397
6. Education (E_6)							0.711	0.425	0.289	0.425	0.544	0.411	0.430
7. Area under HYV								0.255	0.570	0.494	0.611	−0.351	0.688
8. Total Cultivators									−0.092	0.151	−0.117		0.141
9. Agr. Wages for Ploughing (wheat equivalent)										0.237	0.218	0.168	0.434
10. Total cropped area											0.850	0.063	−0.279
11. Agr. Labourers												0.503	−0.021
12. Education of Labourers (E_7)													0.383
13. HYV Proportion													

Table 6.3: Analysis of Interdistrict Differences in Agricultural Wages in Panjab and Haryana: 1968—72. Estimated Coefficients of Multiple Regression Equations — Dependent Variable 'Agricultural Wages for Ploughing'

Variables	Equation 1		Equation 2		Equation 3	
	Co-eff.	t-Value	Co-eff.	t-Value	Co-eff.	t-Value
Constant	1.599	9.309	1.690	9.558	1.907	9.948
1. Total Cropped Area	0.396	6.680	0.373	6.240	0.490	6.536
2. HYV Proportion	0.133	8.303	0.113	5.726	0.019	5.751
3. Cultivators	−0.055	5.405	−0.056	5.573	−0.057	5.880
4. Agricultural Labourers	−0.295	5.275	−0.334	5.622	−0.481	5.770
5. Tractors			0.048	1.725	0.050	1.863
6. Education of Agr. Labourers (E_7)					0.067	2.415
$\bar{R}^2$	0.552		0.568		0.603	
F-Value	19.739		16.954		16.365	

negative signs as explanatory variables. In the second equation we introduce the tractor as an additional explanatory variable which raises the
value of $\overline{R}^2$ to 0.568. The coefficient for tractors is positive but not
significant at the 1 per cent level though significant at the 5 per cent
level. The signs of other coefficients do not change but magnitude
alters somewhat. In this equation also all the explanatory coefficients
except tractors are statistically significant at the 1 per cent level. In the
third equation we introduce Education (E_7), which we have defined
as the proportion of agricultural labourers with completed secondary
education. The introduction of this variable in the third equation
changes the magnitudes of the coefficients considerably suggesting that
the education variable in all probability is a relevant factor in explaining interdistrict variation in agricultural wage rates. In this case again
theory suggests 'if the discarding (including) of a variable changes the
regression coefficients of other variables, then it cannot be a super-
fluous variable' (Rao and Miller, 1971, p. 38). The coefficients of the
third equation which includes education of the agricultural labourers
as an explanatory variable are well estimated, the equation is well
estimated and the value of $\overline{R}^2$, by including the education variable,
increases from 0.568 to 0.603. All the coefficients are statistically
significant at the 1 per cent level except the coefficient for tractors
which is significant at the 5 per cent level.

From a priori reasoning, we know that the supply curve of
agricultural labour in the agricultural sector of Panjab and Haryana,
as argued earlier, in all probability has not shifted. Therefore, the
estimated relationship probably represents shifts in equilibrium
points caused by shifts in the demand for agricultural labour. The
elasticity of wages with respect to total cropped area is 0.49, with
respect to high yielding varieties (HYV) is 0.11 and with respect to
education is 0.07. Interestingly enough, the coefficient for tractors, as
an explanatory variable, is positive with an elasticity of 0.05. The two
influences which have a tendency to pull down wages are the supply
factors representing the number of cultivators and the number of
agricultural labourers per 1000 acres of land cultivated. Cultivators
have a negative elasticity of −0.06, while the elasticity with respect to
the number of agricultural labourers is −0.48. This is consistent with
general observation and common sense that one major influence on
the wage rate in the unorganised agricultural sector is the supply of
labour.

The positive and statistically significant coefficient of education
among agricultural workers suggests that even in the unorganised

labour market with conditions of near perfect competition, the quality differences embodied in educational differences get reflected in wage differentials in different districts of Panjab and Haryana. If the statistical coefficient obtained of Education (E_7) is assumed to be the true coefficient then approximately 7 per cent of the differences in wage rates in different districts of Panjab and Haryana can be accounted for in terms of differences in the general education of the agricultural wage labourers.

Notes

1. This was pointed out by many workers in the field and District level administrators. But due to the legal implications under Land Reform laws, there is no official acknowledgement of this general impression. Empirical checks on this are also very difficult.

2. Sinha (1968) in a pioneering paper explored this question in the context of explaining concepts of employment. He measured wages in lbs of wheat as an index of real wages. We propose to follow a similar procedure in this chapter.

3. For details on this problem see Pranab Bardhan (1970).

7 AN EXERCISE IN COST BENEFIT ANALYSIS OF RURAL EDUCATION

Traditionally the cost-benefit analysis of educational programmes have been based either on the 'cultural approach' or on the conventional criteria (with varying degrees of sophistications) of project evaluation using the internal rate of return (IRR). In this chapter we shall argue that both of them are grossly inadequate in the evaluation of educational projects. Economists concerned with project formulation and evaluation generally agree that the 'cultural approach' is subjective and thus does not provide meaningful yardsticks for the evaluation of educational programmes or projects. We shall attempt to show here that the 'objective criteria' of the internal rate of return used in a conventional way would invariably underestimate the potential benefits of education. This exercise is based on data for Panjab and Haryana but the questions raised and the method used seem to have wider application.

The rate of return approach to education has been described in chapter 2 of this study. The usual objections to the use of this technique as pointed out in chapter 2, in addition to the assumptions of marginal productivity theory of distribution, are as follows.

First, this type of analysis usually treats the difference between the earnings of less educated and more educated people as the benefit due to their additional formal schooling. However, these incremental earnings are due not only to additional schooling, but also to other basic differences arising from a varying socio-economic background and from other 'ability' differences generally unrelated to schooling. Therefore, using additional earnings as a measure of the benefits to investment in education exaggerates these benefits.

Second, the use of earnings or wage differentials as the benefit for additional schooling overlooks the impact of unemployment. Significant unemployment may make wages or salaries invalid as the sole measure of benefits from the point of view both of the individual, who allows for the probability of unemployment in his calculations, and of society, which has a certain percentage of graduates, at each level, earning no wages.

Third, cost-benefit analysis assumes that wages are a valid measure of productivity. Even if there is no unemployment, distortions in the labour market may create gaps between wages and productivity. In many developing countries, public sector wages are higher than private sector wages, and union pressure and national manpower policies set wage and hiring guidelines that may be totally unrelated to productivity. To correct for these distortions, we should estimate 'shadow wages' which would prevail in a purely competitive, distortion-free labour market.

Fourth, cost-benefit analysis derives rates of return to investment in schooling on the basis of benefits and costs at the time the data are collected. The rates may measure the return to investments already made, but they may very well not remain valid for further investment undertaken now or in the future, since both wage differentials and costs are likely to change over time. Therefore, the method should offer some theoretically sound way of calculating future rates of return which allows for changes in the benefits and costs of investment in schooling at various levels.

Fifth, cost-benefit analysis can perhaps measure the direct economic return to education investment, but education is justifiable for many other reasons: as a consumer good, enjoyable and worthwhile for both parents and children alike; or as a political good, a means of changing attitudes towards, for example, family planning, national identity, or other socio-political issues. The analysis should therefore take these potential effects of education into account.

Some studies have taken most of their objections into account and gone ahead with the evaluation of educational projects.[1] The two major problems with all such attempts are:

(a) These studies fail to measure 'externality' of education. The exclusion of the external benefits in the cost-benefit studies of education would lead to underestimation of educational benefits.

(b) The distinction between ex ante and ex post is usually blurred. In a static equilibrium framework, when the contribution of education is marginal and leaves productivity of other factors unaffected, this is not a very serious problem. But where education's role is to deal with disequilibrium, the distinction is crucial. We have called education's role to deal with disequilibrium the 'innovative effect' of education. Nelson and Phelps (1966) and Chaudhri (1968, 1972, 1974) had argued that in the context of economic development this component of education is the most important one. Therefore evaluation of educational programmes ought to take into account this aspect. We present one such exercise in the specific context of rural education in Panjab and Haryana. Since our data on costs and benefits are subject to a number of restrictions the exercise ought to be treated as tentative.

Measuring the Cost-Benefits of Education

The cost-benefits of education can be computed either through:

(a) Calculation of the internal rate of return (IRR), or
(b) Calculation of the cost-benefit ratio, given the rate of discount.

The first is more meaningful in so far as it enables us to compare the IRR with alternative projects and also with education in other countries Since most evaluation studies report IRR, it would be more interesting to compute the cost-benefits of education using IRR.

The general procedure for calculating a rate of return to an investment is to find that rate of discount which sets the discounted value of the time stream of its costs equal to that of the time stream of the benefits accruing to it. In equation form:

$$\sum_{i=1}^{n} \frac{Y_i}{(1+r)^i} = 0$$

$$\text{where } i = 1 \ldots . n \qquad (7.1)$$

where,

Y_i = The difference in year (i) between the net costs and net
    benefits of additional education
  r = The internal rate of return
  n = The length of the expected work life in years

Costs The costs of education borne by the private individual are different from those borne by the society. When we measure society's costs and benefits we get social cost-benefits of education while relating private costs to private benefits gives us the private cost-benefits of education.

The private costs of education consist of fees paid, if any, cost of books and stationery, travelling costs and earnings foregone during the period spent in the acquiring of education (schooling). The last one is the most important component of the private costs of education. For our calculations we assume that in rural areas of Panjab and Haryana the earnings foregone by school children differ according to the age group and are as below:

Age Group	Schooling Level	Earnings by workers in the Age Group
6–11	Lower Elementary (called Primary)	Nil
11–14	Upper Elementary (called Middle)	1/4th of the average annual wage of Permanent Labourers
14–16	Higher Secondary	1/2 of the average annual wage of Permanent Labourers

Since very few children in the age group 6 to 11 in rural areas of Panjab and Haryana work,[2] private costs of schooling up to the end of primary school consists of the cost of books and stationery only. Every village in the area has a Primary School and education up to Primary level is free and compulsory. Therefore there are no travelling costs or school fees.

In the age group 11 to 14 years about 12 per cent of the children are reported to be part-time workers.[3] Since the school year in these areas has roughly 180 working days, the earnings foregone by children in this age group cannot be higher than one-fourth of the average annual wage rate for permanent agricultural workers. The proportion of children in the age group 14 to 16 reported to be working is higher but the school year for this group also is about 180 days in a year. Moreover there is no area in Panjab where a secondary school is located at a distance greater than 3 miles. This enables secondary school children to stay with their families in the village and commute daily to the school and back either on foot or using a push bike. This enables them to participate in the family's farming and other economic activities during long vacations (which usually coincide with the periods of peak labour demand) and over the weekends. Thus the earnings foregone by children in this age group cannot be more than one-half of the adult's annual wage for a permanent agricultural worker.

The costs of providing education were computed by the National Commission on Education (1964–66) and per student costs in the State of Panjab and Haryana are reported in Volume 2 of this report.[4] These are as follows:

Total Per Student Cost Per Year, Panjab: 1961–2 (Rs.)

Primary Schools	Rs. 29.3
Class I–IV	
Middle Schools	Rs. 43.7
Class V–VIII	
Secondary Schools	Rs. 59.1
Class IX–XI	

The costs of books, stationery and travelling were estimated by Nallagounden (1966). Combining all these sources the private and social costs of primary, middle and secondary education are summarised in Table 7.1.

Table 7.1: Annual Cost of Education in Panjab and Haryana: 1961-2 (Rs.)

Private/Social Class	Primary I—IV	Middle V—VIII	Secondary IX—XI
Private:			
School Fees	Nil	Nil	Nil
Books and Stationery	20	20	120
Travelling	Nil	30	60
Earnings Foregone	Nil	360	540
Total Private Cost (Rs.)	20	440	720
Cost of supplying schooling State/Public Authority/ Institutional Cost	117	175	177
Total Social Cost (Rs.)	137	615	897

Benefits In 1961-2 in Panjab and Haryana, the benefits of rural education could not have been lower than the direct contribution of education in production in the farming households as estimated in production function studies based on 1038 cultivating households reported in chapter 5 of this study.[5] But this is largely the 'worker effect' of education as argued earlier. Some of the inputs like chemical fertilisers have been used partly because of the superior information field of the production agent and the marginal contribution of fertiliser use has been attributed to fertilisers since both education and fertilisers are included as explanatory factors in the production function. To this extent educational benefits as measured in a production function are underestimated. Moreover the 'externality' of education has also not been taken into account. On the other hand if we take a gross measure of education's impact as represented by the following equation:

$$Y = f(E) \tag{7.2}$$

where,

    Y = Gross Value of agricultural produce
    E = Level of education.

These relations have been estimated and reported using interdistrict data in chapter 3. This measure of educational impact would definitely *overestimate* it because the contribution of factors related with education would also be attributed to education. The true contribution would be somewhat higher than the contribution estimated for production functions based on household data but lower than the gross measure mentioned above. But these estimates of educational impact are in a static equilibrium framework, that is, this is the contribution of education if the production and input pattern continues to be that observed in the cross section data.

In chapter 3 we have observed that the introduction of a high yielding variety of wheat had significantly changed the relationship between education and agricultural productivity. The change of slope during 1961 to 1972 was estimated and reported in table 3.3. If we attempted an estimate of educational benefits while planning education for this region in 1960-61 and had prior information about the introduction of HYV seed we would have included a part of the educational benefits due to faster diffusion of new technology embodied in HYV seed by farming households with education. But like the gross measure of 1961, the change of slope of education and productivity relationships is not only the contribution of education. Faster diffusion has been possible because farmers with education had a superior information field and also had access to credit, capital and the other input requirements of the HYV package. This enabled them to adopt the package which has given us the change of slope in the relationship between education and agricultural productivity. If we had access to data relating to farming households for the post-Green Revolution period similar to that for the early sixties, we could have compared the coefficients and the marginal product of education of 1961 and, say, 1971. But such data are not available. The Farm Management Studies for Panjab for the years 1967-8, 1968-9, and 1969-70 do not report the educational levels of agricultural workers in the farming family or that of its head. Therefore, we have to make some heroic assumptions about the additional benefits of education due to (a) externalities, and (b) innovations caused by the Green Revolution. These assumptions need not unduly worry us because the point of the whole exercise is to illustrate that in a dynamic agriculture, innovations like the Green

Revolution should not be treated as a once-for-all occurrence and therefore the educational benefits should include the benefits due to the
innovative effect of education. The benefits streams under different
assumptions would be:

(i) The effects of primary education directly accruing to the
farmers are estimated in the production function estimates (reported in
chapter 5) and comes to Rs. 107 per year. The indirect benefits of
primary education due to education workers' participation in
institutions like co-operatives etc. which is an 'externality' of education
are computed from the relationship between education and
agricultural productivity as reported in chapter 3.

We assume that three-quarters of this additional indirect benefit is
due to factors associated with education and only one-quarter of these
benefits is due to education itself. It gives us an additional amount
of Rs. 16 per year. The total direct and indirect effects of primary
education would be Rs. 123 in the situation of stable agriculture of
1961 in this region.

(ii) The benefit of secondary education accruing directly to the
household comes to Rs. 200 per year. The indirect benefits namely the
'Externality', using the same assumption that one-quarter of the
benefits are due to the indirect benefits of education, we get the value
of indirect benefits to be Rs. 129 per year. This gives us a total, direct
and indirect, benefit of secondary education of Rs. 329 per year. Due
to the introduction of high yielding variety seed and the other related
innovations, the productivity increases amount to an annual rate of
16 per cent from 1961 to 1972 in this region.

In chapter 3 we examined the relationship between education and
agricultural productivity and also measured the change of slope of the
relationship between education and agricultural productivity. This is
reported in table 3.8. If we assume that one-quarter of the change of
slope of the education-productivity relationship was due to the
incidence of secondary education in the rural areas, we find that the
additional educational benefits of secondary education come to
Rs. 500 per year.[6] We have called this the 'innovative effect' of
education. In 1971 the total economic benefits of secondary education
including the worker benefits, the allocation benefits and the
innovative benefits, come to Rs. 829 per year.

We assume that the average worker with primary or secondary
education is able to participate in the work force for a period of 30

years. This is realistic because the average expectancy of life is 47 years in this area and a student completes Secondary education at the age of 16. If we allow one year for periodic withdrawal from activity due to morbidity, a worker would have an active working life of 30 years.

Using the costs and benefits, private and social, as discussed above, we computed the internal rate of return to Rural Education in Panjab and Haryana using equation 7.1. The results are reported in Table 7.2.

Table 7.2: Private and Social Rate of Return to Rural Education in Panjab and Haryana

	Costs (Rs.)		Internal Rate of Return	
	Private	Social	Private	Social
1. Primary Education (E_2)	20	137		
(i) Benefits assumption				
(a) Direct benefits				
included			534%	78%
(ii) Benefits assumption				
(b) Direct and indirect				
included			435%	90%
(iii) Benefits assumption				
(c) Total benefits				
including innovative				
effects			N.S.	N.S.
2. Secondary Education (E_3)	1160	1512		
(i) Benefits assumption (a)			17%	13%
(ii) Benefits assumption (b)			17%	22%
(iii) Benefits assumption (c)			71%	55%

We find that the return to rural education, as expected is higher for society than for the individual. This is because of a large component of 'external' benefits of education. The returns to primary education as viewed from the 1961 point of view of society are 90 per cent. The returns of secondary education in the stable agriculture of 1961, on the basis of direct benefits only are 13 per cent for society and 17 per cent for the individual. When we include the indirect benefits, the social return increases to 22 per cent while the private return remains 17 per cent, because indirect benefits do not accrue to the individual. When we include the benefits of education in an economic situation like that of the Green Revolution, we find that the private returns come to the staggering figure of 71 per cent while the social returns come to 55 per cent. The innovative effect of education changes the cost-benefit ratios and IRR significantly.

As pointed out earlier the actual magnitudes are not very important.[7] The point which we want to emphasise is that the conventional method of cost benefit analysis of rural education which has taken into account only the direct benefits gives a social rate of return of just 13 per cent whereas the total benefits of education are some multiple of this figure.

Non-significance of the relationship between productivity and primary education in the post-Green Revolution period does not imply that primary education has no economic benefits. It only suggests that the benefits of primary education have become so diffused that most of it is an externality which we have not been able to capture in our statistical measures. Moreover primary education is the foundation on which we build successfully higher levels of school education. The economic benefits of mere literacy could not be measured statistically for similar reasons even using the 1961 data. This suggests that in a dynamic situation primary education is not enough, sustained school education up to secondary level has a high pay off.

Thus we find that in the evaluation of educational projects relating to rural areas of under-developed countries the use of a static equilibrium framework is inadequate and can be totally misleading in situations like the Green Revolution. We need to do a lot of work in this area to be able to develop stable and meaningful yardsticks for the evaluation of educational projects.

Notes

1. Heinrich and Carnoy (1972) for example have computed cost benefits of education in Kenya taking most of these points into account.
2. See Census 1971, Population Tables.
3. See Census 1971.
4. In 1964–66, this was a single state of Panjab. It was bifurcated into two states of Panjab and Haryana in 1967.
5. Since we have serious doubts about the equality of wages with the marginal product of labour at macro level, we measure 'contribution to production' in a production function rather than wages as a measure of educational benefits.
6. The assumption that one-quarter of the change of education productivity relationship would be due to *education only* is not far from reality because we have seen, in chapters 3 and 4 of this study, that adoption of high yielding variety

seed, development of co-operative societies and the use of chemical fertilisers are all related with secondary education, and these are the elements which have caused the Green Revolution.

7. In fact one could introduce a number of improvements in the measures of costs and benefits of education, if recent and more detailed data were available.

8 CONCLUSIONS AND POLICY IMPLICATIONS

The role of education in agricultural production as pointed out in chapters 1 and 2 is multifarious. The educational impact on production is direct as well as indirect and diffused. We developed conceptual distinctions between various aspects of educational impact, namely, the innovative effect, the allocation effect, the worker effect and the externality of education. We also pointed out in chapter 2 that measuring the relationship between education and agricultural productivity at different levels of aggregation would internalise the externality of education to some extent.

It was argued in chapter 2 that education is both the cause and the result of higher agricultural productivity. A single equation relationship postulated in chapter 3 explored the impact of education on agricultural productivity, the use of some yield raising inputs and the expansion of institutional facilities like the membership of co-operative societies. In estimating all these relationships a causal chain was hypothesised i.e. it was assumed that education of the farm workers influences productivity, use of yield raising inputs etc. The farming family's acquisition of education involves costs (even when the state provides it free). There is the opportunity cost and other expenses and the ability to bear these costs depends on the level of productivity and wealth holding of the farming family. Therefore in the long run, a higher level of agricultural productivity would influence the demand for education. Thus the demand and supply of education both would have positive slopes. Use of cross section data for estimating these relationships would leave the identification problem, in its strict sense, unresolved.

We handled the identification problem to some extent in chapter 4 when we used a simultaneous equation system in which the level of Agricultural productivity, use of chemical fertilisers and demand for education were treated as endogenous variables.

Since we were not sure of the relevant definition of education we had defined education in seven alternative ways (see chapter 1). These alternative definitions were not entirely independent of each other, for example (E_3) and (E_6); (E_1) and (E_4) were to a large extent overlapping. E_1 and E_3 represented the incidence of literacy and secondary education respectively among all agricultural workers, while

E_4 and E_6 related to cultivators only. But the relationship between literacy and elementary education could be independent of each other or it could be complementary. This depends upon the factors that lead farming families to terminate the acquisition of education after literacy (E_1) or Elementary Education (E_2) or go on to further education. Since we did not explore the factors influencing demand for education in detail in this study, we treated all these definitions of education independently of each other. We also defined these different measures of education as the proportion of farm workers with the relevant level of education. We abstained from defining it as a premium for the educated workers in the total labour force because we believe that the educated worker is qualitatively different from the uneducated farm worker as has been argued in chapter 1, and therefore his contribution differs from his uneducated counterpart in an economic sense. Hence we refrained from creating efficiency units of labour using education as a corrective for efficiency.

The statistical exercises reported in chapter 3 lead us to the strong presumption that during 1961 to 1972 the relationship between education and agricultural productivity changed considerably; that of literacy became weaker with the growth, the use of HYV wheat and that of secondary education became stronger in this region. The basic relationships between 1961-2 and 1971-2 seem to have changed, as revealed by Chow tests, but have been stable between 1967-8 and 1971-2.

The relationship between the use of chemical fertilisers, a proxy for innovations, and education also follows a pattern similar to that of the level of agricultural productivity. The relationship with secondary education is positive and significant for each of the years under study but gets stronger after 1965-6.

The results of the factor analysis and multiple correlation analysis reported in chapter 3 indicate that the single most important explanatory factor in the growth of productivity in the agricultural sector of Panjab and Haryana has been the rise in the intensity of cropping which is highly correlated with the use of tubewells, chemical fertilisers and the level of education, in particular the secondary education of cultivators.

The statistical results of the simultaneous equation system reported in chapter 4 indicate that even when education is used as one of the endogenous variables its impact on the use of chemical fertilisers (the innovative effect in our definition) is positive and significant. Education's impact on the level of agricultural productivity is also positive and significant in the first equation of the simultaneous equations system where use of fertilisers is also included as one of the explanatory variables. This suggests that the worker and allocative effect of education is also positive and significant in the period and the region under study.

The results of the farm level production functions reported in chapter 5 indicate that the education of the head of the cultivating family and other agricultural workers in the family is a relevant factor in production even in the pre-Green Revolution period before 1965-6 to which the data pertains. The marginal product of a year of education in the production function estimates turns out to be Rs. 153 for the head of the cultivating household and Rs. 107 for the agricultural workers in the family for a single year. This, in effect, is the worker effect of education as has been pointed out in chapter 2.

In chapter 6 we explored the relationship between agricultural wages and the level of education of agricultural labourers. It was found that 7 per cent of the interdistricts' wage differential can be attributed to the difference in the incidence of secondary education among agricultural wage earners.

The major policy conclusions that emerge from our statistical exercises are that:

General education up to secondary level (i.e. 10 years of conventional schooling) among cultivators has an impact on the diffusion of technology, and agricultural productivity in the wheat belt of India (Haryana and Panjab States). The causal chain has been tested using a simultaneous equations system, and the direction of causation seems right.

The impact of secondary education (10 years of conventional schooling) increased markedly between 1961 and 1972, suggesting that returns from secondary education rise with the coming in of new technology of the type embodied in the Green Revolution.

Just literacy and lower primary education among cultivators in the situation represented by the Green Revolution in Panjab and Haryana do not explain the diffusion of technology, suggesting that in a dynamic agriculture, with a technology of the Green Revolution type, mere literacy is not enough. Sustained rural education up to secondary school level is required.

This does not suggest that elementary education is not important and relevant for regions with technological conditions requiring use of inputs with which farming communities are already familiar. For example Chaudhri (1968) reported a positive and statistically significant relationship between elementary education and agricultural productivity for all regions of India for 1961 and also positive association between literacy and agricultural productivity and modern inputs in other regions but no association between literacy and productivity or inputs in Panjab and Haryana for 1961. This could partly be due to substitution between literacy and informal education or agricultural extension. These results need to be compared with those obtained from other regions for the recent period.

Even in the unorganised labour market in the agricultural sector of Panjab and Haryana, wages among landless agricultural labourers are positively influenced by differences in their level of education, in particular secondary education.

We have not explored questions relating to the content of education or the technology of education. An improved content for agricultural modernisation and a better technology of education needs to be investigated and experimented with for formulation of rural education policy.

Our exercise suggests that rural education among farm workers is, in all probability, a relevant and important factor, for agricultural modernisation. The diffusion of Green Revolution technology in Panjab and Haryana has been facilitated by secondary education (10 years of schooling) of the conventional type among the farmers of the region.

We examined the limitations of the conventional cost-benefit methodology based on static equilibrium framework used in the evaluation of the calculation programmes in chapter 7 and suggested that for formulation and economic evaluation of Rural Education programmes the allocative effects and externality of education should be taken into account. A lot of research work is required to develop stable and objective yardsticks to measure the educational impact for use in economic evaluation of Rural Education programmes.

REFERENCES

Arrow, K. J., 'The Economic Implications of Learning by Doing',
Review of Economics and Statistics, Vol. 29, 1962.

Bailey, F. G., '*Caste and the Economic Frontier*', Manchester, University
Press, 1959.

Bardhan, Pranab, 'Agricultural Wages among Landless Labourers',
Economic and Political Weekly, Bombay, Review of Agriculture,
1970.

Becker, G. S., *Human Capital: A Theoretical and Empirical Analysis
with Special Reference to Education,* Princeton University Press,
1965.

Bell, Clive, 'Acquisition of Agricultural Technology: Its Determinants
and Effects', *Journal of Development Studies*, Vol. 9, October 1972.

Chaudhri, D. P., *Education and Agricultural Productivity in India*, PhD
Thesis, University of Delhi, April 1968.

Chaudhri, D. P., 'Education in Production in Modernising Agriculture
in Asian Under Developed Countries', Research Quarterly, Vol. 1,
No. 2, January 1972.

Chaudhri, D. P., 'Rural Education and Agricultural Development –
Some Empirical Results from Indian Agriculture' in Foster and
Shiefield (eds.), *International Year Book of Education 1974 –
Education and Rural Development,* Evans Bros., London, 1974.

Datar, B. N., Paper submitted to All India Seminar on Agricultural
Labour.

Eckaus, R. S., 'Economic Criteria for Education and Training', *Review
of Economics and Statistics*, Vol. XLVI, No. 2, May 1964.

Evenson, Robert, 'Research Extension and Schooling in Agricultural
Development' in Evenson and Kislev, *Investment in Agricultural
Research and Extension*, pp. 163–84, London, 1973.

Gadgil and Dandekar, V. M., *Primary Education in Satara District*, Asia
Publishing House, Bombay, 1955.

Govt. of India, Report of *Expert Committee on Unemployment Estimate*
New Delhi, 1971.

Griliches, Z., 'Contribution of Education in Production and Growth
Accounting' in Lee Hansen (ed.), *Education and Income*, National
Bureau of Economic Research, New York, 1970.

Griliches, Z., 'Notes on the Role of Education in Production Functions
and Growth Accounting', paper contributed to Conference on

Education and Income organised by National Bureau of Economic Research, Wisconsin University, 1969.

Griliches, Z., 'Research Expenditure, Education and Aggregate Agricultural Production Functions', *American Economic Review*, LIV, December 1964.

Harbinson, F. H. and Myres, C. A., *Education, Manpower and Economic Growth: Strategies of Human Resource Development*, McGraw-Hill, New York, 1964.

Harker, B. R., *Education, Communication and Agricultural Change: A Study of Japanese Farmers*, unpublished PhD Thesis, University of Chicago, June 1971.

Haung, D., *Regression and Econometric Methods*, McGraw-Hill, New York, 1971.

Herdt, R. W., 'Resource Productivity in Indian Agriculture', *American Journal of Agricultural Economics*, Vol. 53, No. 3, August 1971.

Kahlon, A. S. *et al.*, *The Dynamics of Panjab Agriculture*, Panjab Agricultural University, Ludhiana, 1971.

Kao, H. C., 'Disguised Unemployment in Agriculture: A Survey' in Eicher and Witt (eds.), *Agriculture in Economic Development*, McGraw-Hill, New York, 1964

Karam, Singh, *Resource Adjustment Possibilities and Resource Use Efficiency in Panjab Agriculture,* PhD Thesis, PAU, Ludhiana, 1971, Mimeo.

Kislev, *Explorations in Agricultural Production Functions*, PhD Thesis, University of Chicago, 1967.

Klein, L. R., *Introduction to Econometrics*, Prentice Hall of India, New Delhi, 1965.

Kuh, *Capital and Investment*, Rotterdam, North Holland, 1971.

Mehra, Shakuntala, 'Surplus Labour in India Agriculture', *Indian Economic Review*, Vol. 1 (New Series), No. 1, April 1966.

Nelson, R. R. and Phelps, E. S., 'Investment in Humans, Technological Diffusion and Economic Growth', *American Economic Review*, LVI, No. 2.

Parulekar, R. V., *Literacy in India*, 1939.

Planning Commission, Government of India, *Draft Outline—Fifth Five-Year Plan*, Section 12.7, 1973.

Raj Krishna, 'Unemployment in India', *Indian Journal of Agricultural Economics*, Vol. XXVIII, No. 1, January—March 1973, pp. 1—23.

Raj, K. N., *Economics of Bhakra Nangal Project*, Asia Publishing House, Bombay, 1959.

Rao, P. and Miller, R. L., *Applied Econometrics*, Eastern Economy Edition, New Delhi, 1970.

Rogers, E. M. and Shoemaker, F. F., *Diffusion of Innovations,* New York, The Free Press of Glencoe, 1971.

Roy, *et al., Diffusions of Innovations in India*, Bowling Green, USA, 1972.

Sahota, G. S., 'Efficiency of Resource Allocation in Indian Agriculture', *American Journal of Agricultural Economics*, pp. 584–655, August 1968.

Saini, G. R., *Economics of Farm Management with Special Reference to Some Selected Holdings in Uttar Pradesh*, PhD Thesis, Delhi University, January 1973.

Saini, G. R., 'Resource Use Efficiency in Agriculture', *Indian Journal of Agricultural Economics*, April–June 1969.

Saini, G. R., 'Holding Size, Productivity and Some related Aspects of Indian Agriculture', *Economics and Political Weekly – Review of Agriculture*, 26 June 1971.

Schultz, T. W., *Transforming Traditional Agriculture*, New Haven, Yale University Press, 1964.

Schultz, T. W., A Reply to A. K. Sen 'Surplus Labour in India – A Critique of Schultz's Test', *Economic Journal*, September 1967.

Sen, A. K., 'Economic Approach to Education and Manpower Planning', *Indian Economic Review*, April 1966.

Sen, A. K., 'Surplus Labour in India: A Critique of Schultz's Statistical Test', *Economic Journal*, pp. 154–60, March 1967.

Sen, A. K., 'Dimensions of Unemployment in India', *Mainstream*, Vol. 12, No. 20, 12 January 1974, New Delhi (8th Convocation Address – Indian Statistical Institute, Calcutta).

Sinha, J. N., 'Unemployment in a Developing Economy', *Indian Journal of Agricultural Economics*, Vol. XIII, No. 2, April–June 1968.

Thiel, *Aggregation of Economic Relations*, North Holland, Rotterdam, 1957.

Tinbergen, J. and Correa, 'Quantitative Adaption of Education to Accelerated Growth', *Kyklos,* Vol. XV, 1962.

Tinbergen, J. and Bos, H. C., 'A Planning Model of Educational Requirements of Economic Development', in OECD, *Econometric Models of Education*, Paris, OECD, 1964.

Welch, F., 'Education in Production', *Journal of Political Economy*, January 1970.

APPENDIX A: ANNOTATED BIBLIOGRAPHY OF STUDIES RELATING TO THE ROLE OF EDUCATION IN AGRICULTURAL PRODUCTION

Adamski, I., 'Improved Peasant Farming as a Result of the Social and Professional Activities of the Farmers', *International Journal of Agrarian Affairs*, Vol. V, No. 4, July 1969, pp. 97–102. Supplement on the First IAEE Inter European Seminar Proceedings.

The study is based on a sample of 2735 farms in the Plock District of Poland. The conclusions are that in the planned economy of Poland, the incentive system induces the farmers to adopt improved methods. The adoption of improved methods is quicker among farmers who are subscribing to a paper or a journal or those who read books on agricultural production in comparison to those who do not do so. Thus, this study underlines the importance of the information field in adoption of improved methods and considers education as a means of dissemination of information.

Adelman, Irma and Colladay, Frederick, L., 'A Systems Analysis of Investment in Education for Economic Development and Social Political Modernisation', a paper presented at the *Russel Sage Foundation Seminar on Quantitative Techniques for the Analysis of Social Change*, February 1969 (Mimeographed).

The paper studies the relationship of education to political, social and economic development. Systems analysis is used to explore these questions. The results suggest an appropriate role for education in national modernisation based on US development. To compare the results for a developing country the study uses data for Morocco. Using linear programming the study comes to the conclusion that the role of education is crucial in promoting the growth of the agricultural sector and the national economy.

Ardito-Barleta, N., *Returns of Agricultural Research in Mexico*, unpublished PhD thesis, University of Chicago, 1971.

This is an agricultural study of the impact of the Mexico-Rockerfeller Research Programme in Mexico during the period 1943 to 1964. The general conclusion is that the project has had a very high pay off. The points of interest from the role of education in agricultural production are:

(a) greater attention to the extension of research results to farmers could have increased the pay off of the project;

(b) it is suggested that part of the explanation for the differential adoption rates, and hence the differential pay off in respect of wheat and corn, may lie in the level of training and education of the corn farmers *vis-à-vis* the wheat farmers. These proportions indicate complementarity relation between research and extension, and research and education.

Barbaris, C., 'Education and other human factors in the economy of a settlement project (Sardinia) Italy', *International Journal of Agrarian Affairs*, Vol. V, No. 4, July 1969, pp. 161–74. Supplement on the First IAEE Inter European Seminar Proceedings.

The study relates to 120 observations from enterprises established by the Nurra region land reform project in Italy. Various characteristics of the farmers like their age, education, size of holding, type of farming activity and regional characteristics are examined. The study also explores the educational performance of the children from these 120 settler families. The correlation between farm income and scholastic achievement (both in marks and number of failures) is positive and significant, more operative among boys than among girls. The general conclusion is that a child's performance in the school to some extent depends on the intrinsic (i.e. within the family) education on the part of the parents which in turn has a significant effect on farm productivity. The education of a farmer is found to be significantly related to his performance in his economic enterprise.

Bessell, J. E., 'Measurement of the Human Factor in Farm Management', *International Journal of Agrarian Affairs*, Vol. V, No. 4, July 1969, pp. 36–44. Supplement on the First IAEE Inter European Seminar Proceedings.

The study relates to a group of dairy farmers in the East Midlands of England in 1961 and a simultaneous equations model is used to interpret data for a period of eight years (1959 to 1966). The following two simultaneous equations are estimated:

$$P_n = \dot{a}_1 T_n + \dot{a}_2 M_n + \dot{e}_1$$
$$M_n = \dot{b}_1 T_n + \dot{b}_2 C_n + \dot{b}_3 S_n + \dot{e}_2$$

where P_n is a productivity index, T_n is an intensity index, M_n is the operating efficiency index, C_n is a complexity index and S_n is the potential operating efficiency index. A flow chart represents the activities involved in grass-land dairy farming. The statistical results reveal that a general measure of efficiency cannot diagnose the ills or virtues of bad or good management. Statistical predictions tied well with actual events of the period.

Castillo, Gelia, 'Education for Agriculture', *The Malayan Economic Review*, Vol. 16, No. 2, October 1971, pp. 6–24.

This paper is devoted specifically to agriculture in the Philippines. The author surveys agricultural education in the Philippines as it existed in 1970 in terms of the number of institutions, students, educational expenditure within the agricultural sector and the utilisation of skilled people trained in these institutions. The current and anticipated needs for bachelor's, master's and PhD degrees is reported from an unpublished PhD thesis by M. D. Leonor Jr., *High Level Manpower needs in agriculture as reported by employers*, University of Philippines College of Agriculture, 1969. The study concludes by suggesting some new approaches to education for agriculture such as relating applied research and agricultural demonstration plots to educational institutions and emphasising the need for special training for agricultural extension agents.

Chaudhri, D. P., *Education and Agricultural Productivity in India*, PhD Thesis, University of Delhi, April 1968.

This study provided the first clear-cut distinction between the allocative and the worker effect of education among farm workers in the agricultural sector. He used a production function at various levels of aggregation to internalise the externality of education. The empirical part of the study relates to cross section data for the year 1958 to 1961 for the Indian agricultural sector at different levels of aggregation using interhousehold, intervillage, interdistrict and interstate data. The study concludes that the level of agricultural productivity is significantly related to the level of education in Indian agriculture for the cross section of data examined.

Chaudhri, D. P., 'Education in Production in Modernising Agriculture
    in Asian under-developed countries', in *Agriculture and Economic
    Development in Asian Perspective*, Japan Economic Research
    Centre, Tokyo, June 1972 (Proceedings of an international seminar
    held in Tokyo and Hakone in September 1971).

The paper deals with the role of education in pursuing different strategies of agricultural development in the Asian region. The author argues
that in the absence of basic changes in the rural education policy the
strategy of agricultural development in different countries of Asia,
irrespective of the pronouncements of policy makers, will be bimodel
leading to increased rural inequality. The statistical results of educational impact as observed in Indian agriculture by the author in his
earlier work are compared with those obtained in Japanese agriculture
by Harker (1971) and in other studies relating to other parts of Asia.
The paper concludes that education is one of the crucial inputs in creating
a dynamic agricultural sector.

Chaudhri, D. P., 'Rural Education and Agricultural Development –
    Some Empirical Results from Indian Agriculture' in Foster and
    Shiefield (eds.), *International Year Book of Education 1974 –
    Education for Rural Development,* Evans Bros., London, 1974.

The study examines various components of educational impact in the
agricultural sector and goes into the details of the effects of the farmer's
education on his ability for innovation and allocation. The empirical
results reported are from the author's PhD thesis 'Education and
Agricultural Productivity in India', University of Delhi, April 1968.

Dandekar, V. M., 'Planning in Indian Agriculture', *Indian Journal of
    Agricultural Economics*, Vol. 22, No. 1, January-March 1967,
    pp. 7–23.

This is a presidential address delivered on the occasion of the 26th
Annual Conference of the Indian Society of Agricultural Economics.
The author analyses the reasons for failure of planning in the field of
agriculture in the first part of his paper. The second half is devoted
to policy prescriptions which are based on the following three
elements: 1. to educate and improve the farmer as a farmer; 2. to
reorganise the production apparatus in agriculture so as to enable the
farmer to take better care of his land and inputs like water resources;

and 3. to create appropriate institutions in order to improve decision-making in agriculture.

Of these three, the first, education, is considered to be a major bottleneck for the proposed new strategy. According to the author, education of the farmer would help in changing his attitude to nature. Once education is used to explain the working of nature and indicates possibilities of modifying and harnessing it in the interests of man, much of his traditional attitudes to nature would get modified automatically. Secondly, education will clarify the distinction between traditional knowledge and modern science wherever it influences production ability. In particular, it will emphasise the fact that modern science is experimental while traditional knowledge is largely authoritative. Lastly, education will emphasise the difference between a traditional and the modern attitude to certain aspects of human life and endeavour. This would explain the existence of relations between man and man in the process of production and how and why these need to be changed in the interests of production efficiency. According to him these three aspects of education would prepare the farmer for a transition from traditional agriculture to modern agriculture.

Elstrand, E., 'Norwegian Experience from Extension Work in Farm Management', *International Journal of Agrarian Affairs*, Vol. V, No. 4, July 1969, pp. 91–5. Supplement on the First IAEE Inter European Seminar Proceedings.

This study reports the relative earnings among family workers according to farm size and level of education. Interestingly, it comes to the conclusion that farmers educated at the agricultural schools consistently have higher earnings than those without education. The differential is lowest where farm size is less than 10 hectares and is highest where farm size is over 30 hectares. (This difference is to be logically expected because with the larger farm size management factor becomes more important and thus the innovative and the allocative effects of education acquire larger magnitudes. See Chaudhri (1968).)

Evenson, Robert, *The Contribution of Agricultural Research*, unpublished PhD thesis, University of Chicago, 1968.

The study was primarily concerned with identifying the impact of research and extension on agricultural output. After estimating the relevant lags the author regressed agricultural output on research and extension and on education, besides other variables. The conclusion was that research and extension had yielded high rates of return in US agriculture. Although the interactive effects of research, extension and education were normally recognised, the study did not include an investigation of this aspect, especially of the effect of such interaction on the contribution of schooling to productivity. The primary focus of investigation was the contribution of research and extension to agricultural output holding the education level constant.

Evenson, Robert, 'Research, Extension and Schooling in Agricultural Development' in Evenson and Kisley, *Investment in Agricultural Research and Extension*, Yale University, 1973 (mimeograph), pp. 163–84.

In this paper the author examines, using production functions, the inter-relationships between education, extension and research and explores the theoretical implications of this inter-relationship. The theoretical model is empirically tested on data relating to different geo-climatic regions of the world for the year 1965. The study concludes that research has very high interdependence in different sub-regions of the world. International agencies can and should be guiding the international systems towards a more efficient mix as well as encouraging resources transfers from rich to poor sub-regions.

Evenson, Robert, 'Technology generation and Agriculture', unpublished paper, Yale University, 1973 (mimeograph).

This study relates to the significance of research and extension in Indian agriculture. The study is based on state level data and estimates a production function relating total factor productivity to research, extension, weather, time and region, and concludes that the rate of return on research in Indian agriculture is high.

Fane, George, *The Productive Value of Education in U.S. Agriculture*, PhD thesis, Department of Economics, Harvard University, 1974.

This study attempts to measure the productive value of education in agriculture using data from the 1964 US Census of Agriculture for counties in Indiana, Illinois, Iowa and Missouri. An unrestricted Cobb-Douglas production function is used in which education is

included as a determinant of effective labour input. The coefficient
of education is statistically significant and positive. The estimated
coefficients imply that the marginal return to an extra year in school,
evaluated at the sample mean, is about US $200 in each subsequent
year worked. The study also attempts to estimate the cost of failing
to achieve full cost minimisation and hence an estimate of the value
of education in reducing information inaccuracy. The results show
that education significantly helps farmers to reduce excess costs. The
estimated marginal value of an extra year of education in reducing
excess costs in one limited context is about US $100 in each
subsequent year worked.

Griliches, Zvi, 'Research Expenditure, Education and the Aggregate
Agricultural Production Function', *The American Economic
Review*, Vol. IV, No. 6, December 1964.

This is the first attempt at estimating an aggregate agricultural
production function which specified education as an explicit explanatory variable. The data used are for farm averages for 39 states and
deflated by various national price indices with 1949 as a base. The
data related to 1949, 1954 and 1959. An unrestricted Cobb-Douglas
production function was used. Apart from the conventional input
variables, education, a combined variable of research and extension are
used. The estimates are presented both with education research and
extension variables and without these variables. It is shown that the
explanatory power of the function improves when the education,
research and extension variables are included in the function. This
study succeeds in explaining part of the unexplained residue in a
growth accounting framework.

Griliches, Zvi, 'A Note on Capital Skill Complementarity', Department of Economics and Graduate School of Business, *Report*,
No. 6905, University of Chicago, January 1969 (mimeograph).

In this note the author explores the question: Is skill or education of
labour complementary with physical capital? For examining this
hypothesis, he sets up equations assuming constant returns to scale.
He uses cross sectional data for the US and assumes that the price of
'skill' has been largely equalised by the mobility of the educated
labour. He tests this hypothesis on data relating to two digit
manufacturing industry by states which gives him a total number of

261 observations. He finds the relationship between raw labour and physical capital to be negative while skill and physical capital are positively related. This suggests that in all probability skills are complementary to physical capital.

Haller, Thomas Elmer, *Education and Rural Development in Columbia*, unpublished PhD thesis, Purdue University, June 1972.

The study attempts to evaluate the effectiveness of the primary school system as it exists in rural Columbia and to analyse the way in which the schooling contributes to farm family income. A production function similar to that used by Chaudhri (1968) is used as an underlying theoretical model. The coefficients of education in the agricultural production function at the regional level provide a measure of the benefits of rural education while the cost of rural education is measured in a straightforward manner as direct and indirect costs at market prices. The rate of return, private and social, from schooling investments is calculated for four different regions in rural Columbia. The results indicate that the rate of return is significant and high in one of the four regions, interestingly the region with the highest rate of change in the agricultural sector. For the remaining three regions, the innovative and allocative effects of education appear to be insignificant. The study concludes that in a situation of long term equilibrium in traditional agriculture, education's role is not very significant while in a dynamic agriculture, education's contribution is positive and significant. Thus educational investment in rural schooling in areas of dynamic agriculture has a very high rate of return.

Harker, Bruce Rogers, *Education, Communication and Agricultural Changes — A Study of Japanese Farmers*, unpublished PhD thesis, University of Chicago, June 1971.

This study is based on data relating to 3000 Japanese farmers for the year 1966 and examines interhousehold and intercommunity data with a view to specifying and testing an analytical model of the relationship between education, communication behaviour, agricultural innovations and agricultural production. The relationships are explored first in terms of differences among individual farmers and then in terms of aggregate (community) differences among farm localities. Regression equations are used in both analyses; the resultin standardised regression coefficients are used in the causal model. These analyses are supplemented by factor analysis of the data for communities, cutting through identification problems to delineate distinctive patterns among communities in the measurement of education, the adoption of agricultural innovations and income variables. His statistical analysis leads him to conclude that the number of times a farmer consults an agricultural extension agent in a year is related positively to his education attainments and that of his father. His findings are similar to those of Chaudhri (1968) for Indian farms.

Harker, Bruce Rogers, 'The contribution of schooling to Agricultural Modernisation: an empirical analysis', unpublished paper, University of Chicago, 1973.

The study examines the role of extension and education in Indian agriculture and compares it with that of Japan. The conclusions of the study are: 1. in so far as schooling contributes to the development of literacy and of general communication skills, it can make an important contribution to agricultural modernisation; 2. an equally great contribution, too, can be made by the mass media and by a system of agricultural extension services. According to the author the schooling of the farmers and extension services are mutually supporting but are also capable of independently providing a stimulus to agricultural change.

Harrison, Bennett, 'Education and Unemployment in the Urban Ghetto', *American Economic Review*, Vol. 62, No. 5, December 1972, pp. 796–812.

This paper is based on the author's PhD thesis completed in Pennsylvania University. This is a unique and extremely interesting study based on data produced by the US Department of Labour for the year 1966 from city ghettos urban employment service. A total of 37330 people's records form the statistical basis of this study. The specific questions examined are whether unemployment rates in urban ghettos are significantly higher than those prevailing in the economy as a whole; and secondly, even with the same years of schooling, whether the median individual weekly wage for people living in ghettos is significantly lower than that of people in other sections of the community. The lowest paid individuals are black with less than ten years of schooling and live in ghettos. Earnings of all ghetto dwellers with or without education are lower than those of their counterparts living outside ghettos. The study convincingly argues that lower rates of return to education in ghettos is because of poorer quality of education and labour market discrimination. Therefore the policy suggestion is to raise educational investments and to take steps towards reducing labour market discrimination.

Herdt, Robert W., 'Resource Productivity in Indian Agriculture', *American Journal of Agricultural Economics*, Vol. 53, No. 3, August 1971, pp. 517–21.

This note reports estimates of the aggregate production function for India's agriculture and compares these with the Hayami's meta-production function estimates, with the studies by Griliches for the United States and with district level analysis for India by D. P. Chaudhri. The reported results are similar to those of Chaudhri indicating a small but positive effect of education on agricultural production in India while in the United States the effect of education is larger than that in India. This is because Indian agriculture in the pre-Green Revolution period did not have many innovation possibilities available to the farming families.

Hesselbatch, J., 'Adoption of new Working Routines and the Speedy Adaptation of the Labour Input', *International Journal of Agrarian Affairs,* Vol. V, No. 4, July 1969, pp. 45–7. Supplement on the First IAEE Inter European Seminar Proceedings.

This is a short note on the use of labour over a ten year period (1956-7 to 1965-6), among farm groups with less than 50 acres in different parts of West Germany. The adaptation is found to be related to the education of the farmers.

Huffman, Wallace, *The Contribution of Education and Extension to Differential Rates of Change,* unpublished PhD thesis, Department of Economics, University of Chicago, September 1972.

The study is based on a random sample of 122 observations relating to a cross section of counties from Illinois, Indiana, Iowa, Minnesota and Ohio (different States of USA) for the period from 1959 to 1964. The empirical model is a partial adjustment model with a variable adjustment coefficient which consists of two algebraic forms, a logistic function and an exponential function relating farm operator education, and agricultural extension with other input and output variables. A two stage estimation procedure is used to estimate the model. First, the optimum rate of nitrogen fertiliser used for each quantity is estimated for 1964 and 1959 for a demand function. The parameters of the demand function are estimated from the parameters of an estimated production function. Second, the estimated value for the optimum rate for nitrogen in 1964 for each county is substituted into the adjustment equation and the parameters of the variables of the adjustment function are estimated. The study concludes that farmers with more education are clearly aware of a wider range of information sources than those with less education, and the more educated farmers are assumed to be more efficient at processing information and reaching decisions. Consequently, for the same incentive to produce 'good decisions' in a dynamic environment, farmers with more education adjust faster. The marginal effect of the extension service is found to be positive. When the extension service is a major source of technical information to educate groups, farmers with more education benefit more than the less educated ones from the extension service. A major finding of the study is that economic variables, farm operators' education, the extension service activity and the mean acres of farm explained part of the differences in the rate of adjustment to the current optimum for the usage of nitrogen fertiliser on farms for the period from 1959 to 1964 in US agriculture.

Huffman, Wallace E., 'Decision making: The role of education', American Journal of Agricultural Economics, February 1974.

The paper relates to a single dimension of the type of allocative efficiency, namely the adjustment of the farmers to the change in optimum quantity of a single input, nitrogen fertiliser, in corn production in some parts of the USA. The author uses a partial adjustment model with a variable adjustment coefficient; the rate of adjustment to disequilibrium in the use of nitrogen fertiliser between 1959 and 1964 is explained by economic variables. The data is from different counties in Illinois, Indiana, Iowa, Minnesota and Ohio. The results suggest that: 1. Decision makers with more education can more quickly grasp changes and adjust more quickly and accurately to them; 2. An increase in the availability of information eases the gathering and processing of information when adjustment is required; 3. Scale economies exist in using information. The paper is extracted from the author's PhD dissertation entitled 'The Contribution of Education and Extension to Differential Rates of Change', University of Chicago, 1972.

Khaldi, Nabil, *The Productive Value of Education in US Agriculture, 1964*, unpublished PhD thesis, Southern Methodist University, January 1973.

The study attempts to examine the productive value of education of the farmers in the context of two effects:
(a) A 'Worker Effect', defined as the increased output per unit change in education holding other factor quantities constant.
(b) An 'Allocative Effect', that is, the increased level of education within the dynamics of United States agriculture, which enhances the farmers' ability to acquire and decode information about production characteristics, as well as about costs of other factor inputs. An agricultural production function with education and research variables in addition to other inputs (land, machinery, labour, livestock, seed, feed and fertiliser) are used to explain change in output using an unrestricted Cobb-Douglas production function. The empirical results indicate that the elasticity of education is positive in the estimated production function, providing evidence that the worker effect and the allocative effect are positive. The positive coefficients of education and research activity support the hypothesis that both belong in the production function. The returns to education are inversely related to the cost of failure to maximise *ex post* profits while research productivity is directly related to these deviations. The farm size as well as size efficiency relationships are positively related to the productivity of education and research activity. These results indicate that both inputs are increasing functions of scale. The study concludes that education in production makes the farm managers more productive than their less educated counterparts.

Lockwood, William, 'Employment, Technology and Education in Asia', *The Malayan Economic Review*, Vol. 16, No. 2, October 1971, pp. 6–24.

In this paper the author provides a concluding summary of the Conference on Employment Problems in East and South-East Asia held at the University of Singapore from 22 to 28 May 1971. The issue discussed in the conference related to the definition of various concepts and measurement problems in this area. The country variations and the regional perspective are summarised from different papers. The importance of a development stage in labour absorbing is underlined from the experience of Japan, South Korea and Taiwan. Creation of jobs and the level of productivity depends on the level of technology. Questions regarding the use of technology in South-East Asia are briefly discussed. The need for education and manpower for particular levels of technology is outlined.

Malanicz, Z., 'The Influence of Managers' Qualifications Upon the Efficiency of Work of Peasant Farms', *International Journal of Agrarian Affairs*, Vol. V, No. 4, July 1969, pp. 55–8. Supplement on the First IAEE Inter European Seminar Proceedings.

The paper reports data from Polish agriculture from 1130 farms for the year 1957-8. These farms are divided into two categories: the first category consists of farmers who had fourth grade primary school education or more. Efficiency of farm operations is measured in terms of productivity per unit of labour input and labour requirement per unit of output. The statistical explorations in this paper reveal that along with a rise in the level of education of the farmer a considerable increase in efficiency of work took place. Secondly, the increase of production per hectare of agricultural land took place with a decrease of the labour force on all farms but the rate of decrease of labour force was higher among more educated farmers.

Malanicz, Z., 'The Influence of Managers' Qualifications Upon the Material and Financial Expenditure on Peasant Farms', *International Journal of Agrarian Affairs*, Vol. V, No. 4, July 1969, pp. 111–14. Supplement on the First IAEE Inter European Seminar Proceedings.

This paper reports statistical results from 1135 Polish farms. The statistical results indicate that the expenditure per hectare of agricultural land is highest among farms of less than three hectares and is lowest among farms of over 14 hectares but within each farm group the educational level of the farmers is significantly related to the level of investment per hectare. The general conclusion is that the fixed and circulating capital for fertilisers, seed and purchased fodder increased more quickly than total expenditure. All these were higher among the farmers with education.

Malassis, Louis, *The Rural World: Education and Development*, The

UNESCO Press, Paris; Croom Helm, London, 1976, pp. 127.

The work is divided into three parts. Part one describes the relationship between development and education, part two deals with the integration of the rural world into the development process and part three deals with the integration of the rural world into the overall educational system. The monograph does not question or examine the role of education. Education is considered important for developments and the creation of an educational system is discussed in this study.

Manteuffel, R. and Zuk, J., 'The Influence of the Educational Level of State Farm Managers upon Results of Farming', *International Journal of Agrarian Affairs*, Vol. V, No. 4, July 1969, pp. 115–20. Supplement on the First IAEE Inter European Seminar Proceedings.

This study relates to 123 state farms from Polish agriculture. The farms are cross classified according to the educational level of the managers, their age, years of experience, farm size etc. The results indicate that between 1960-1 and 1966-7 state farm managers having academic agricultural education supplied 25 to 30 per cent more marketed surplus as compared to managers with primary education only. Output per worker also was found to be higher on the state farms with managers having secondary or higher level of agricultural education. The profitability indices of these farms also varied according to the level of education of the farm managers, suggesting the conclusion that the educational level of the farm managers is a significant factor in determining output per acre, productivity per worker and index of profitability.

Millikan, Max. F., 'Education for Innovation' in *Restless Nations: A Study of World Tensions and Development*, Dodd, Mead & Company, New York, 1962.

The author explores in some detail the role of education in innovation and the need to develop more economical educational methods which are specially geared to encourage innovations. The need for new methods of language instruction in developing countries is underlined. The emphasis is on an attempt to develop a kind of education which changes individuals' attitudes towards nature, develops a problem solving approach and fosters a desire for search and the selection of new solutions. This is the first detailed and cogent attempt at explaining what education is required to do in the development process of the less developed countries.

Nelson, R. R. and Phelps, E., 'Investment in Humans, Technology Diffusion, and Economic Growth', *American Economic Review*, May 1966, pp. 69–75.

The authors in this paper suggest that '. . . in a technologically progressive or dynamic economy production management is a function requiring adaptation to change and . . . the more educated a manager is the quicker will he be to introduce new techniques of production . . . Educated people make good innovators so that education speeds the process of technological diffusion.' (page 70) The testable models which they have built around the hypotheses suggest that the return to education is greater, the faster the advance of the level of theoretical technology. The payoff to education will be higher in situations where the store of available technology adopted in practices is larger. Their study is based on theoretical reasoning only and suggests these testable propositions which are similar to those of Schultz, namely that education will have a higher payoff in a technologically dynamic economy where there is scope for the exercise of discretionary abilities, adaptability and decision making faculty.

Orkisz, T., 'Premise for Investigating the Qualities of a Farm Manager by the Results of his Farm', *International Journal of Agrarian Affairs*, Vol. V, No. 4, July 1969, pp. 131–9. Supplement on the First IAEE Inter European Seminar Proceedings.

This paper examines qualities of the farm manager which could influence the efficiency of the farm operations. The qualities examined were number of years of agricultural practices, the number of years of work on a given farm, the age of the manager and the education level of the manager. These questions were examined for a sample of 2723 state farms in different parts of Poland. The results indicate that about 20 years of agricultural practice, between 4 and 5 years' work on a given farm, an age of 45 years for a manager and a level somewhere between primary and secondary agricultural education were found associated with the maximum profitability index, highest production and yield per hectare.

Rati Ram, *Education as a Quasi Factor of Production: The Case of*

India's Agriculture, PhD thesis, University of Chicago, December 1976.

The study suggests that schooling lowers the marginal costs of information and/or raises its marginal benefits and thus provides an incentive to the more educated producers to acquire a greater amount of information. Such reduction in costs, rise in benefits and the consequent increase in information are the major sources of efficiency of more educated persons. Thus, it is argued, schooling has mainly an indirect impact on productivity and in this sense it may be regarded as a quasi factor of production. From these basic postulates several implications are derived and it is shown how the proposed framework can explain rather neatly quite a few well known phenomena in regard to the effect of schooling. Some of the implications are specialised to India's agriculture of the 1960s, and the predictions are tested with the district and state level data for the years 1960-1 and 1970-1.

Rheinwald, H., 'Some Remarks on Farmers' Ability and Attitudes', *International Journal of Agrarian Affairs*, Vol. V, No. 4, July 1969, pp. 31—5. Supplement on the First IAEE Inter European Seminar Proceedings.

In this study the author refers to empirical work of Buhler (in the German language) which examines the relationship between professional achievements, the intelligence level of the farmer and the extent of the extension effort. The conclusion is that in farmers' behaviour there is no one single overall motive, but a multiplicity of motives integrated into an indivisible whole made up of striving for social prestige and being afraid to take risks, looking for security and straining to avoid a change of habits: all these together determine behaviour and result in a line of action. Thus the importance of the human factor in agricultural entrepreneurship is underlined in the study.

Foster and Shiefield (eds.), *International Year Book of Education 1974: Education for Rural Development*, Evans Brothers, London, 1974.

The 1974 issue of the International Year Book of Education was exclusively devoted to the role of education in rural development. In addition to the editors' introduction there are 20 papers specially written for the Year Book dealing with various aspects of the relationship between education and rural development. Authors include

T. W. Schultz, Robert Evenson, D. P. Chaudhri, F. Welch and Bruce Harker among others.

Schimmerling, H., 'The Work of the Manager in an Agricultural Enterprise', *International Journal of Agrarian Affairs*, Vol. V, No. 4, July 1969, pp. 191–9. Supplement on the First IAEE Inter European Seminar Proceedings.

The study relates to agricultural co-operatives in Czechoslovakia. It is found that agricultural co-operatives which do not have graduates on their management have poor economic performance as compared to those who have persons with college education in managerial positions. The study explores hours put in each day by different categories of management persons and finds that Directors of farms devote 11.14 hours per day while Chief Economists contribute only 9.17 hours per day. Managers with education spent more time in preparation for consultancy and meetings within the enterprise. This probably explains why personal incomes of workers, production and output per worker is higher in co-operatives with educated managers.

Schultz, T. W., 'Under-investment in the Quality of Schooling in the Rural Farm Areas' in *Increasing Understanding of Public Problems and Policies*, Farm Foundations, Chicago, Illinois, 1964.

The author explains that the change in incidence of education among white and non-white workers between rural and urban areas from 1940 to 1962 has been very uneven. He also points out that the participation of persons from rural areas particularly from the Southern States in higher education activity has been slower than the national average. The enrolment in colleges in 1960 also indicates that 48 per cent of urban high school graduates attend college while only 32 per cent of the rural high school graduates continue their further education. His explanation of these differences is differences in the quality of education. This is reflected in public expenditure per pupil in school education. Per pupil expenditure in richer states was $576 while in poorer states it was $241 for the year 1962-3. According to the author this underinvestment in poorer states and in rural areas is because farm people do not have adequate political control of the public schools which their children attend. They are up against discrimination: schooling is seen mainly as consumption, like a car for teenagers — expensive, time consuming, keeps them away from doing useful work —

and that is why it must be held in check; farm people simply cannot afford the amount and quality of schooling, that is assumed to be warranted in the study. They lack the means and finally they lack the necessary information to make optimum decisions with respect to the amount and quality of schooling that is called for. As a policy prescription he suggests motivation and opportunity to attend schools for farm people should be increased by conscious public action.

Schultz, T. W., 'The Rate of Return in Allocating Investment Resources to Education', *Journal of Human Resources*, Vol. II, No. 3, Summer 1967.

In this paper Schultz summarises the results and issues involved in various studies that use a rate of return in allocating resources in education. He suggests that profiles of earning from education are relatively accurate and reliable while estimates of factor costs of education are far from satisfactory. The estimates of private rates of return are becoming useful indicators of particular ex post disequilibria in the supplies of educated labour. The social rates of return are not in good repair either theoretically or empirically. Finally, he points out that we know very little about the tendency to equilibrium or about the responses of students and schools to the relative rates of return.

Schultz, T. W., 'Optimum Investment in College Instruction: Equity and Efficiency', *Journal of Political Economy*, Vol. 80, No. 3, Part II, May–June 1972, pp. S2–S30.

In this paper Professor Schultz, a leading authority on the subject, provides an excellent review of studies on the economics of education, in particular the aspects that affect productivity and efficiency. He explores questions which he calls economic growth-education puzzles. The first question he asks is that growth theory should explain sources of the investment opportunities that explain the growth process. There is some evidence to indicate that creation of human and non-human capital at particular rates led to a particular level of growth. The second question he discusses is the rise in particular cost and allocative benefits of education associated with growth. He discusses the allocative benefits of education as reported by Chaudhri (1968-9), Welch (1970), Freeman (1971) and others. On the other hand, economic growth had led to the enlargement of a student's capacity for educational finance and benefits. This has led to a rightward shift in the demand curve. Thus a situation of equity-efficiency quandary has arisen. He concludes by stating that the statistical evidence on some of the assertions which assume that students behave as economic firms, is in the nature of statistical hypotheses that await more complete testing.

Schultz, T. W., 'The Value of the Ability to Deal with Disequilibria', *The Journal of Economic Literature*, Vol. XIII, No. 3, September 1975, pp. 827–46.

Professor Schultz is one of the leading experts on the role of education in agricultural modernisation. In this paper he summarises and synthesises various studies completed in the US and other developed countries as well as in the developing countries. The relationship of education in production, consumption and fertility decisions within the household are discussed. Referring to the studies completed by Chaudhri (1968, 1973), Welch (1970), Haller (1972), Huffman (1972), Harker (1971) and others he points out the crucial role of education is that it provided the decision maker with an ability to deal with disequilibria. This paper is an important starting point for anyone interested in pursuing research in this area. He divides the paper into seven sections. Section 1 deals with concepts of human abilities, Section 2 examines the equilibrating activities of individuals to regain equilibrium, Sections 3 and 4 deal with static equilibrium and its comparison with dynamic disturbances. The last three sections deal with the role of entrepreneurship, elements of a theory describing the value of ability to deal with disequilibria and substantial evidence from researchers mentioned above. These three sections are pertinent to the role of education in agricultural production and the evidence cited overwhelmingly supports the contention.

Van Den Ban, A. W., 'The human factor in Farm Management. Some Research Evidence from the Netherlands', *International Journal of Agrarian Affairs*, Vol. V, No. 4, July 1969, pp. 79–90. Supplement on the First IAEE Inter European Seminar Proceedings.

This study is based on farm management data for the year 1957 for Dutch farmers. The socio-economic characteristics of different adoptor categories were examined. The conclusions based on statistical findings, are that education influences the adoption rate probably via information which the farmers get from the mass media. Before adopting a new practice farmers invariably have a personal discussion with somebody they consider competent. The local extension officers usually consider educated farmers well informed and thus willingly offer their time for discussion. Usually such farmers have more resources and higher status in their communities than those who adopt these practices later.

Welch, F., 'Education in Production', *Journal of Political Economy*, Vol. 78, No. 1, January–February 1970, pp. 35–59.

The paper examines the reasons for the expansion in the supply of skilled labour in the agricultural sector of the United States. Three alternative explanations for relative wage determination among skilled classes in agriculture are advanced. According to him the incentive for acquiring a college education is based on dynamic considerations of changing technologies. Using a production function the relative wage differentials among various categories of skilled workers in US agriculture are explained. The study concludes that the rates of return to investment in schooling has remained high which probably explains the reasons why the pressure of rapidly rising average educational level has continued. The basis for continued high premiums for skills in agriculture is rapidly changing technology, thus suggesting that the innovation effect and the allocation effect of educational impact is significant and present in US agriculture.

Welch, Finis, 'Relationships between income and schooling', unpublished paper NBER, January 1973.

The first part of the paper is devoted to summarising the issues raised in earlier studies on the relationship between income and schooling. The reasons as reported in various studies explaining the differences in individual incomes are summarised. The factors like differences in ability and the measurement of ability are also examined in detail. The second part of the paper explores causal factors in black-white income differences for the years 1959 to 1966 in the US economy. The macro level explanation of the relationship between income and schooling as reported by Griliches, Welch, Khaldi and Huffman are summarised with an emphasis that all this evidence clearly points out that education's role is primarily allocative. The paper concludes with a suggestion that much more research should be devoted to establishing linkages between micro and macro level relationships.

Yudelman, M., Butler, G., Banorji, R., *Technological Changes in*

Agriculture and Employment in Developing Countries, Development Centre Studies, Employment Series No. 4, OECD, Paris, 1971.

The study is divided into three parts. Part I examines features of employment in traditional agriculture, the process of technological change in agriculture and the effect of technological change on the structure of traditional agriculture. Part II is devoted to case studies of technological changes and labour utilisation at a farm level. Examples from Japan, Taiwan and Mexico are taken to examine

1. land augmenting innovations and the demand for labour at farm level,
2. the introduction of mechanisation, and
3. selective mechanisation.

The examination of hypotheses at the aggregate level is based on circumstantial evidence from Japan, Taiwan and Mexico. Part III of the study is devoted to the international transfer of agricultural technology and the policy implications of these transfers. It is suggested that land augmenting technologies tend to increase the demand for labour at the farm level. The demand for labour at the farm level is also influenced by the rate of diffusion of innovation. The study concludes by stressing that very little empirical analysis of the effects of technological changes on the demand for labour both on and for farms is available for the developing countries.

APPENDIX B: SOURCES OF DATA

The statistical data used in this study were collected from various
government agencies and research institutions. The details of the
sources are as under.

1. For the Interdistrict Study of Panjab and Haryana States

Gross Value of Agricultural Produce

This series is computed for each district of Panjab and Haryana by
aggregating the area under production of 12 principal crops multiplied
by their respective prices for the period 1960-1 to 1971-2. The statistics
relating to area and yield are collected from the Directorate of
Economics and Statistics, Ministry of Food and Agriculture, Government of India. Information relating to agricultural prices of these
principal crops is collected from the Directorate's study *Agricultural
Prices in India* and for the district series from *Statistical Abstracts* of
Panjab and Haryana for different years.

Agricultural Inputs

Statistics relating to the intensity of land use, irrigation, fertiliser use
and tubewells is obtained from *Statistical Abstracts* of Panjab and
Haryana for different years for district series and from the Directorate
of Economics and Statistics' records for state level observations.
Statistics on tractors and tubewells for the year 1971 were obtained
from the files of the Offices of the Economic and Statistical Advisers to
the Governments of Panjab and Haryana.

Bullock Power

These data are collected at five year intervals in the Livestock Census.
Information pertaining to 1961 to 1966 are obtained from the
Livestock Censuses of 1961 and 1966. The Livestock Census of 1971
was postponed by one year due to the Indo-Pakistan War of 1971.
Information for this period is still unpublished and was obtained from
the Offices of the Economic and Statistical Advisers to the Government
of Panjab and Haryana.

Cultivators and Agricultural Labourers

Information relating to cultivators and agricultural labourers is published in Part 2 B-II (i) of the 1961 Census for the year 1961; and in population tables Part B of the 1971 Census for the year 1971. Statistics for the intervening years are interpolated on the basis of data for these two end points.

Education of the Farm Workers

For the purposes of this study we define education in four alternative ways: literacy, elementary education, secondary education and higher education including degrees and diplomas. Educational characteristics of cultivators and agricultural labourers for the year 1961 are reported in Part B-III tables of the 1961 Census. Similar information was obtained from the records of the Census authorities for the year 1971. Information for the intervening years was interpolated on the basis of these two end points.

Extension Effort

We define extension effort as the number of extension workers per thousand cultivators in each district of Panjab and Haryana. This information was obtained from the Departments of Agriculture and the Governments of Panjab and Haryana respectively. Unfortunately, this was available only for one year, 1971.

Co-operative Societies and Co-operative Credit

A questionnaire was mailed to the Registrar of Co-operative Societies in Panjab, Haryana and other states of India. Information relating to the number of co-operative societies, membership of each society and annual financial turn-over was obtained through this questionnaire for the years 1960-1 to 1970-1.

Enrolment in Rural Education

Statistics relating to educational enrolment in rural areas were obtained from Departments of Education, the Governments of Panjab and Haryana, the Statistical Section of the Central Ministry of Education and the Education Division of the Planning Commission.

2. For Interhousehold Study

The Agricultural Economics Research Centre, University of Delhi, carried out intensive investigations into the input-output relationship of all the households in some selected villages of Panjab, Haryana and UP in their Continuous Village Survey series. We obtained information relating to the number of workers, gross value of agricultural produce, area cultivated, area irrigated, fertiliser used, cost of cultivation and educational characteristics of workers from the original household questionnaire used in their village surveys in the second round of surveys conducted during 1961 to 1964. Information for each cultivating household was specifically for one single agricultural year (July to June for that year). We obtained information relating to 1038 households from 19 villages belonging to the wheat belt of Panjab, Haryana and UP.

APPENDIX C: STATISTICAL TABLES

Table A.1: CHOW Test for Stability of Coefficients (1961 to 1972)
Interdistrict Data for Panjab and Haryana (N = 15)
Dependent Variable : Yield Per Hectare

| Year | Independent Variables Alternative Measures of Education | | | |
	E_2	E_3	E_5	E_6
1961	0.136881	0.121956	0.165054	0.125782
1962	0.132941	0.090534	0.166790	0.099976
1963	0.324087	0.173888	0.375381	0.166023
1964	0.337494	0.152583	0.375167	0.147438
1965	0.423890	0.247547	0.438032	0.232069
1966	0.361383	0.169091	0.370201	0.153439
1967	0.315198	0.198617	0.314132	0.182476
1968	0.897383	0.543275	0.893182	0.496972
1969	0.342760	0.259659	0.342991	0.238975
1970	0.452413	0.289591	0.450316	0.253956
1971	0.512249	0.374856	0.514481	0.337976
Σ ESS (Q_2)	4.236679	2.621597	4.405727	4.706082
Total SS (Q_1) (For Pooled Data)	7.932051	5.417818	8.220170	5.072349
$F = \dfrac{(Q_1 - Q_2)/2}{Q_2/(165 - 4)}$	70.21477*	85.862087*	69.69625*	6.265189*

$F(2,200) = 4.71$ at 1% level
*Significant at 1% level

Table A.2: CHOW Test for Stability of Coefficients (1961 to 1972)
Interdistrict Data for Panjab and Haryana   (N = 15)
Dependent Variable : Fertiliser per Hectare

Year	Independent Variables Alternative Measures of Education			
	E_2	E_3	E_5	E_6
1961	0.798058	0.537598	1.213271	0.560265
1962	1.046041	0.404276	1.654409	0.555028
1963	1.056059	0.406757	1.405643	0.481279
1964	1.206909	0.421898	1.491045	0.512536
1965	1.519422	0.487458	1.747921	0.594657
1966	1.950014	0.714423	2.125562	0.767046
1967	2.069265	1.016593	2.142098	1.042951
1968	2.869644	1.629685	2.877722	1.554737
1969	2.524612	1.581482	2.515226	1.480584
1970	2.582096	1.723503	2.572996	1.578380
1971	3.159467	2.291917	3.160470	2.093982
Σ ESS (Q_2)	18.451587	11.215590	22.906363	11.176445
Total SS (Q_1) (For Pooled Data)	33.010946	19.167167	36.242205	19.023416
$F = \dfrac{(Q_1 - Q_2)/2}{Q_2/(165 - 4)}$	63.51911*	57.07252*	46.86625*	56.51897*

$F(2,200) = 4.71$ at 1% level.
*Significant at 1% level

Table A.3: CHOW Test for Stability of Coefficients (1967 to 1972)
Interdistrict Data for Panjab and Haryana   (N = 15)
Dependent Variable : Yield Per Hectare

Year	Independent Variables Alternative Measures of Education			
	E_2	E_3	E_5	E_6
1967	0.315198	0.198617	0.314132	0.182476
1968	0.897383	0.543275	0.893182	0.496972
1969	0.342760	0.259659	0.342991	0.238975
1970	0.452413	0.289591	0.450316	0.253956
1971	0.512249	0.374856	0.514481	0.337976
Σ ESS (Q_2)	2.520003	1.665998	2.515102	1.510355
Total SS (Q_1) (For Pooled Data)	2.653583	1.750676	2.628692	1.594223
$F = \dfrac{(Q_1 - Q_2)/2}{Q_2/(75 - 4)}$	1.88	1.80	1.60	1.97

$F(2,70) = 3.13$ at 5% level
Difference Statistically Not Significant

Table A.4: CHOW Test for Stability of Coefficients (1967 to 1972)
Interdistrict Data for Panjab and Haryana   (N = 15)
Dependent Variable : Fertiliser Per Hectare

Year	Independent Variables Alternative Measures of Education			
	E_2	E_3	E_5	E_6
1967	2.069265	1.016593	2.142098	1.042951
1968	2.869644	1.629685	2.877722	1.554737
1969	2.524612	1.581482	2.515226	1.480584
1970	2.582096	1.723503	2.572996	1.578380
1971	3.159467	2.291917	3.160470	2.093982
Σ ESS (Q_2)	13.205084	8.243180	13.268512	7.750634
Total SS (Q_1) (For Pooled Data)	13.990101	8.405346	13.890990	7.868424
$F = \dfrac{(Q_1 - Q_2)/2}{Q_2/(75 - 4)}$	2.11	0.70	1.67	0.54

$F(2,70) = 3.13$ at 5% level
Difference Statistically Not Significant

Table A.5: Zero Order Correlation of Variables of the Two Stage Least Square Estimates of the Model for Education and Productivity in Panjab and Haryana : 1968-9 to 1971-2   (N = 60)   (Variables in Logs)

Variables (a)	Gross Value of Agr. Produce (1)	Total Cropped Area (2)	Area sown more than once (3)	Fertilisers (Y_2) (4)	Agr. Labour (5)	Tubewells (6)	Education (Y_3) (7)	HYV Area (8)	Cultivators (9)	No. of students in classes (IX—XI) (10)	$\hat{Y}_1$ (11)	$\hat{Y}_2$ (12)	$\hat{Y}_3$ (13)
1. Gross Value of Agr. Produce (Y_1)		0.805	0.827	0.713	0.911	0.687	0.736	0.870	0.844	0.653	0.973	0.732	0.878
2. Total Cropped Area			0.919	0.264	0.875	0.351	0.486	0.521	0.963	0.485	0.827	0.275	0.583
3. Area sown more than once				0.378	0.887	0.495	0.589	0.600	0.885	0.652	0.859	0.383	0.690
4. Fertilisers (Y_2)					0.608	0.754	0.674	0.861	0.392	0.492	0.723	0.962	0.846
5. Agr. Labour						0.556	0.727	0.706	0.923	0.686	0.937	0.632	0.871
6. Tubewells							0.659	0.792	0.451	0.624	0.706	0.784	0.790
7. Education (Y_3)								0.717	0.597	0.680	0.753	0.734	0.834
8. HYV Area									0.584	0.563	0.895	0.896	0.860
9. Cultivators										0.602	0.868	0.408	0.715
10. No. of Students in classes											0.671	0.511	0.815
11. $\hat{Y}_1$												0.752	0.902
12. $\hat{Y}_2$													0.879
13. $\hat{Y}_3$													

Table A.6: Test for Statistical Differences in Coefficient for Different Measures of Education

	Dependent Variable YIELD PER HECTARE				Dependent Variable YIELD PER WORKER				Dependent Variable FERTILISER PER HECTARE			
	1961	1966	1971	Pooled	1961	1966	1971	Pooled	1961	1966	1971	Pooled
Coefficients												
b_2	0.417	0.689	-0.133	0.999	0.099	0.053	-0.399	0.656	1.678	1.787	-0.071	2.399
b_3	0.304	0.740	0.579	0.868	0.184	0.225	0.074	0.576	1.230	1.892	1.437	2.067
b_5	0.391	0.755	-0.097	1.121	-0.047	0.098	-0.425	0.741	1.616	1.808	0.017	2.607
b_6	0.358	0.988	0.636	0.955	0.181	0.277	0.134	0.640	1.475	1.866	1.538	2.325
Differences in Coefficients												
$b_2 - b_3$	0.113	-0.051	-0.712	0.131	-0.085	-0.172	-0.473	0.080	0.448	-0.105	-1.508	0.332
$b_2 - b_5$	0.026	-0.067	-0.036	-0.122	0.146	-0.045	0.026	-0.085	0.062	-0.021	-0.088	-0.208
$b_3 - b_6$	-0.055	-0.058	-0.057	-0.087	0.003	-0.052	-0.060	-0.064	-0.245	-0.074	-0.121	-0.158
$b_5 - b_6$	0.032	-0.042	-0.733	0.166	-0.228	-0.179	-0.559	0.101	0.141	-0.158	-1.541	0.382
Standard Error of Coefficients												
SE b_2	0.154	0.326	0.438	0.102	0.200	0.268	0.212	0.102	0.372	0.757	1.088	0.208
SE b_3	0.097	0.150	0.262	0.058	0.124	0.170	0.166	0.066	0.204	0.308	0.647	0.111
SE b_5	0.200	0.375	0.521	0.120	0.238	0.305	0.258	0.119	0.541	0.900	1.290	0.253
SE b_6	0.119	0.150	0.243	0.061	0.155	0.174	0.159	0.070	0.251	0.336	0.605	0.119
t-Values												
$t(b_2 b_3)$ (15 + 15 − 4 Df)	0.6209	-0.1421	-1.3950	1.1121	-0.3611	-0.5419	-1.7571	0.6534	1.0559	-0.1285	-1.1913	1.4086
$t(b_2 b_5)$	0.1030	-0.1349	-0.0529	-0.7744	0.4696	-0.1108	0.0778	-0.5424	0.0944	-0.0179	-0.0521	-0.6351
$t(b_3 - b_6)$	-0.3583	-0.2735	-0.1595	-1.0258	0.0151	-0.2137	-0.2610	-0.6653	-0.7576	-0.1624	-0.1366	-0.9711
$t(b_5 - b_6)$	0.1375	-0.1010	-1.2750	1.2333	-0.8028	-0.5098	-1.8443	0.7314	0.2364	-0.1645	-1.0816	1.3662

b_2 = Coefficient of Ed_2 Hypothesis $b_3 = b_6$

b_3 = Coefficient of Ed_3 Hypothesis $b_2 = b_5$

b_5 = Coefficient of Ed_5 Hypothesis $b_2 = b_3$

b_6 = Coefficient of Ed_6 Hypothesis $b_5 = b_6$

$$t(b_i b_j) = \frac{b_i - b_j}{\sqrt{[SE(b_i)]^2 + [SE(b_j)]^2}}$$

for 26 Degree of freedom.

Table A.7: Explanation of the Growth of Gross Value of Agricultural Produce through Growth of Input Factors — Districts of Panjab and Haryana 1961 to 1972 (N = 15)

Variables		Means	X/Y	$x_3,x_4,x_5,x_6,x_7,x_8,x_9,x_{15}$		$x_3,x_4,x_5,x_6,x_7,x_8,x_9,x_{14}$		$x_3,x_4,x_5,x_6,x_7,x_8,x_9,x_{13}$		$x_3,x_4,x_5,x_6,x_7,x_8,x_9,x_{12}$		$x_3,x_4,x_5,x_6,x_7,x_8,x_9,x_{11}$		$x_3,x_4,x_5,x_6,x_7,x_8,x_9,x_{10}$	
				b Coeff.	Elasticity	b Coeff.	Elasticity	b Coeff.	Elasticity	b Coeff.	Elasticity	b Coeff.	Elasticity	b Coeff.	Elasticity
Gap	y	16.203													
Total Cropped Area	x_3	1.134	0.070	0.575	0.040	0.818	0.057	0.925	0.065	0.584	0.041	0.838	0.059	0.926	0.065
Irrigated Area	x_4	6.757	0.417	−0.109	−0.045	−0.009	−0.004	−0.134	−0.056	−0.125	−0.052	−0.041	−0.017	−0.130	−0.054
Fertiliser	x_5	34.886	2.153	0.110	0.237	0.063	0.136	0.103	0.222	0.106	0.228	0.066	0.142	0.097	0.209
Labour	x_6	0.306	0.019	0.418	0.008	0.404	0.008	0.381	0.007	0.419	0.008	0.383	0.007	0.450	0.009
Bullocks	x_7	0.206	0.013	0.147	0.002	0.184	0.002	0.066	0.001	0.142	0.002	0.167	0.002	0.060	0.001
Oil Engines	x_8	30.898	1.894	−0.028	−0.053	−0.034	−0.064	0.014	0.027	−0.021	−0.040	−0.022	−0.042	0.013	0.025
Tractors	x_9	20.913	1.291	0.040	0.052	0.010	0.013	0.081	0.105	0.000	0.057	0.005	0.006	0.072	0.093
Ed$_1$	x_{10}	−6.431	−0.397											−0.024	0.010
Ed$_2$	x_{11}	7.622	0.470									0.317	0.149		
Ed$_3$	x_{12}	10.008	0.618							0.302	0.187				
Ed$_4$	x_{13}	7.710	0.476					0.016	0.008						
Ed$_5$	x_{14}	6.385	0.394			0.336	0.132								
Ed$_6$	x_{15}	9.258	0.571	0.301	0.172										

Table A.8: Zero Order Correlation — Growth of Input Output
(Interdistrict Data of Panjab and Haryana 1961 to 1972)   (N = 15)

Variables (a)	Gross Agr. Produce (1)	Net Sown Area (2)	Total Cropped Area (3)	Irrigated Area (4)	Fertilisers (5)	Tractors (6)	Labour (7)	Bullocks (8)	Education (E_6) (9)
1. Gross Agr. Produce		0.795	0.870	−0.398	0.683	0.889	0.470	0.401	0.499
2. Net Sown Area			0.868	−0.384	0.492	0.607	0.309	0.328	0.317
3. Total Cropped Area				−0.215	0.411	0.745	0.322	0.367	0.538
4. Irrigated Area					−0.259	−0.423	−0.138	0.061	−0.099
5. Fertilisers						0.657	0.499	0.328	0.046
6. Labour							0.455	0.251	0.229
7. Bullocks								0.043	−0.114
8. Tractors									0.212
9. Education (E_6)									

Table A.9: Explanation of Growth of Gross Value of Agricultural Produce through Growth of Input Factors (Districts of Panjab and Haryana 1961 to 1972) (N = 15)

Dependent Variable GAP	Without Education			Proportion of AGRICULTURAL WORKERS with						Proportion of CULTIVATORS with					
				Completed Primary Education E_2			Completed Secondary Education E_3			Completed Primary Education E_5			Completed Secondary Education E_6		
Explanatory Variables (a)	Coeff. (1)	t-Value (2)	Partial Corr. (3)	Coeff. (4)	t-Value (5)	Partial Corr. (6)	Coeff. (7)	t-Value (8)	Partial Corr. (9)	Coeff. (10)	t-Value (11)	Partial Corr. (12)	Coeff. (13)	t-Value (14)	Partial Corr. (15)
1. Total Cropped Area	0.925	2.970	0.557	0.838	2.807	0.568	0.584	2.036	0.409	0.818	3.063	0.610	0.575	2.089	0.421
2. Irrigated Area	−0.138	−1.017	0.129	−0.041	−0.296	0.014	−0.124	−1.204	0.195	−0.008	−0.068	0.001	−0.109	−1.088	0.165
3. Fertilisers	0.101	1.346	0.206	0.066	0.882	0.115	0.106	1.792	0.349	0.063	0.953	0.132	0.100	1.927	0.382
4. Labour	0.414	1.522	0.249	0.383	1.496	0.272	0.419	1.955	0.389	0.404	1.770	0.343	0.418	2.026	0.406
5. Bullocks	0.063	0.406	0.033	0.167	1.170	0.186	0.142	1.314	0.223	0.184	1.471	0.265	0.147	1.412	0.250
6. Oil Engines	0.014	0.353	0.017	−0.022	−0.487	0.038	−0.021	−0.620	0.060	−0.034	−0.831	0.103	−0.028	−0.815	0.100
7. Tractors	0.077	0.829	0.089	0.005	0.051	0.000	0.044	0.596	0.056	0.010	0.117	0.002	0.040	0.561	0.050
8. Education				0.317	1.403	0.247	0.302	2.295	0.468	0.336	1.985	0.386	0.301	2.485	0.507
$\bar{R}^2$		0.861			0.878			0.914			0.802			0.820	

Table A.10: Relationship between Yield Per Hectare and Education: Time Series Data for Panjab and Haryana (N = 11) 1961-62 to 1971-72

Log Yield/Hectare = Log b_0 + b_1 Log Ed.

District	Education 2			Education 3			Education 5			Education 6		
	b	t-Value	$\bar{R}^2$	b	t-Value	$\bar{R}^2$	b	t-Value	$\bar{R}^2$	b	t-Value	$\bar{R}^2$
Ambala	2.157	7.252	0.821	1.967	7.279	0.823	2.233	7.154	0.817	1.983	7.161	0.818
Amritsar	3.944	13.552	0.943	2.105	12.630	0.935	3.586	11.757	0.925	1.966	11.770	0.925
Bhatinda	4.139	10.309	0.905	2.166	10.110	0.901	3.449	10.109	0.901	1.942	9.883	0.897
Ferozepur	3.611	9.570	0.891	1.988	10.367	8.096	3.943	10.414	0.906	1.998	10.411	0.906
Gurdaspur	3.122	14.025	0.947	1.914	13.967	0.946	2.962	13.603	0.943	1.704	13.562	0.943
Gurgaon	1.487	8.860	0.874	1.014	8.518	0.865	2.212	7.525	0.832	1.299	7.512	0.832
Hissar	1.400	6.272	0.772	1.332	6.272	0.772	1.091	6.132	0.764	1.716	6.131	0.764
Hoshiarpur	2.163	8.767	0.872	1.435	8.815	0.873	2.794	7.719	0.840	1.491	7.721	0.840
Jullundur	2.983	11.091	0.917	2.375	10.752	0.912	3.117	9.499	0.889	2.007	9.531	0.890
Kapurthala	2.201	7.762	0.841	7.120	10.541	0.908	2.166	6.831	0.802	4.547	6.824	0.802
Karnal	2.261	13.147	0.940	1.693	13.593	0.943	2.524	13.597	0.943	1.715	13.596	0.943
Ludhiana	6.885	12.237	0.931	2.464	10.365	0.906	5.792	9.241	0.883	2.066	9.219	0.883
M. Garh	0.791	3.717	0.517	0.694	3.737	0.521	0.991	3.861	0.540	0.837	3.860	0.540
Rohtak	1.273	12.560	0.934	0.860	10.841	0.913	2.025	8.087	0.852	1.127	8.081	0.852
Sangrur	1.874	11.214	0.918	2.136	11.255	0.919	2.105	10.618	0.910	2.316	10.607	0.909

Table A.11: Relationship between Yield Per Worker and Education: Time Series Data for Panjab and Haryana (N = 11) 1961-62 to 1971-72

Log Yield/Worker = Log b_0 + b_1 Log Ed.

District	Education 2			Education 3			Education 5			Education 6		
	b	t-Value	$\bar{R}^2$	b	t-Value	$\bar{R}^2$	b	t-Value	$\bar{R}^2$	b	t-Value	$\bar{R}^2$
Ambala	2.186	6.890	0.805	1.997	7.003	0.810	2.313	7.931	0.847	2.055	7.962	0.848
Amritsar	3.588	12.091	0.929	1.918	11.636	0.924	3.271	11.155	0.918	1.793	11.165	0.918
Bhatinda	3.344	8.280	0.858	1.748	8.115	0.853	2.783	8.087	0.052	1.567	7.960	0.848
Ferozepur	3.371	9.395	0.867	1.845	9.437	0.888	3.633	8.818	0.873	1.841	8.816	0.873
Gurdaspur	3.234	15.085	0.954	1.981	14.708	0.951	3.063	13.926	0.946	1.762	13.819	0.945
Gurgaon	1.680	9.378	0.887	1.145	8.877	0.875	2.491	7.627	0.836	1.463	7.614	0.836
Hissar	1.463	6.288	0.773	1.391	6.289	0.773	1.986	6.148	0.765	1.792	6.147	0.765
Hoshiarpur	2.144	7.416	0.828	1.444	8.367	0.861	2.892	9.459	0.888	1.543	9.459	0.888
Jullundur	2.622	10.380	0.906	2.088	10.116	0.901	2.742	0.101	0.880	1.765	9.131	0.881
Kapurthala	2.322	9.329	0.885	7.395	11.244	9.919	2.303	8.395	0.862	4.834	8.382	0.861
Karnal	2.269	15.250	0.954	1.690	15.152	0.954	2.515	13.353	0.941	1.709	13.351	0.941
Ludhiana	5.375	8.687	0.870	1.911	7.505	0.832	4.474	6.844	0.803	1.596	6.833	0.802
M. Garh	0.989	5.089	0.685	0.867	5.107	0.686	1.228	5.189	0.694	1.037	5.187	0.694
Rohtak	1.683	14.086	0.947	1.137	11.720	0.925	2.647	8.387	0.861	1.486	8.381	0.861
Sangrur	1.384	8.958	0.877	1.576	8.909	0.876	1.564	9.142	0.881	1.721	9.136	0.881

Table A.12: Relationship between Fertiliser per Hectare and Education: Time Series Data for Panjab and Haryana (N = 11) 1961–62 to 1971–72

Log Fertiliser/Hectare = Log a + b Log Ed.

District	Education 2			Education 3			Education 5			Education 6		
	b	t-Value	$\bar{R}^2$	b	t-Value	$\bar{R}^2$	b	t-Value	$\bar{R}^2$	b	t-Value	$\bar{R}^2$
Ambala	5.912	8.910	0.876	5.379	8.752	0.871	5.958	7.078	0.814	5.286	7.045	0.812
Amritsar	9.353	13.401	0.942	4.992	12.501	0.933	8.505	11.672	0.924	4.663	11.680	0.924
Bhatinda	7.756	12.397	0.932	4.060	12.137	0.930	6.450	11.619	0.924	3.634	11.424	0.921
Ferozepur	6.570	12.397	0.932	3.587	12.004	0.928	7.041	10.361	0.905	3.567	10.358	0.905
Gurdaspur	7.180	12.876	0.937	4.394	12.423	0.933	6.783	11.641	0.924	3.902	11.605	0.923
Gurgaon	2.869	15.321	0.955	1.957	13.863	0.945	4.270	10.692	0.911	2.508	10.672	0.910
Hissar	3.563	15.411	0.955	3.389	15.301	0.955	4.799	11.876	0.927	4.332	11.884	0.927
Hoshiarpur	4.395	13.109	0.939	2.891	11.379	0.921	5.533	7.971	0.848	2.952	7.974	0.848
Jullundur	5.702	21.262	0.976	4.546	20.501	0.974	6.002	17.308	0.964	3.862	17.385	0.865
Kapurthala	4.789	13.063	0.939	15.210	18.110	0.967	4.753	11.020	0.916	9.980	11.015	0.916
Karnal	5.623	14.352	0.949	4.215	15.272	0.955	6.298	16.422	0.961	4.279	16.413	0.960
Ludhiana	10.809	20.181	0.974	3.899	17.807	0.966	9.207	15.092	0.954	3.285	15.049	0.953
M. Garh	1.576	10.268	0.904	1.380	10.139	0.902	1.926	9.076	0.880	1.627	9.074	0.880
Rohtak	2.167	8.186	0.855	1.473	7.990	0.849	3.516	7.206	0.819	1.953	7.203	0.819
Sangrur	3.900	15.024	0.953	4.444	15.207	0.954	4.373	13.260	0.940	4.812	13.239	0.940

Table A.13: Agricultural Wages in Kgs. of Wheat per Day in Panjab and Haryana 1961 to 1972 (Agr. Year)   (Ploughing)

District	1960/1	1961/2	1962/3	1963/4	1964/5	1965/6	1966/7	1967/8	1968/9	1969/70	1970/1	1971/2
Ambala	8.59	7.13	6.51	5.90	5.70	5.51	..	5.39	5.71	6.42	6.77	6.70
Amritsar	3.97	3.86	8.06	8.09	6.37	5.99	5.19	6.32	6.93	7.30	8.39	7.92
Bhatinda	8.64	9.01	10.01	8.09	8.01	7.99	7.33	7.40	8.17	8.59	9.86	9.50
Ferozepur	5.66	5.15	5.20	6.36	6.60	6.07	4.46	5.12	6.91	7.72	9.33	8.49
Gurdaspur	4.97	5.56	6.24	7.52	4.43	6.39	4.84	4.24	7.04	6.78	7.16	7.00
Gurgaon	7.25	6.48	6.02	5.37	5.45	4.85	4.83	6.73	8.00	8.88	9.39	8.80
Hissar	7.93	10.86	9.66	7.75	8.37	6.92	4.93	8.55	7.14	8.05	9.12	8.92
Hoshiarpur	5.95	5.15	6.08	5.78	5.43	4.79	3.94	4.83	8.08	7.60	7.81	7.32
Jullundur	6.93	7.39	7.93	6.64	5.65	..	4.17	5.61	6.74	7.34	8.68	8.91
Kapurthala	7.93	..	..	..	9.08	5.59	6.75	7.70	8.82	8.83	9.70	8.52
Karnal	6.25	5.47	5.99	6.44	4.68	3.86	2.58	5.94	6.95	8.67	9.39	8.80
Ludhiana	6.08	6.64	6.50	6.06	7.16	..	6.21	7.23	6.44	7.60	9.54	9.42
M. Garh	9.93	8.06	7.78	8.59	4.84	6.36	9.93	5.05	4.67	5.87	8.05	7.54
Rohtak	..	8.56	8.56	7.51	6.88	5.32	3.62	5.39	6.95	7.71	8.05	8.42
Sangrur	8.72	9.01	10.04	5.43	7.63	7.19	7.19	8.62	8.76	7.78	7.48	8.76
Panjab	7.04	6.77	7.03	6.54	6.19	6.10	5.44	7.09	7.53	8.08	8.62	8.46
Haryana	7.04	6.77	7.03	6.54	6.19	5.46	4.09	6.28	5.91	7.80	8.69	8.50

Table A.14: Agricultural Wages in Kgs. of Wheat per Day in Panjab and Haryana 1961 to 1972
(Agr. Year)   (Sowing)

District	1960/1	1961/2	1962/3	1963/4	1964/5	1965/6	1966/7	1967/8	1968/9	1969/70	1970/1	1971/2
Ambala	8.46	7.18	6.65	6.12	5.05	5.51	..	5.39	5.65	6.42	6.71	7.33
Amritsar	3.97	3.86	8.06	6.36	6.45	5.67	5.19	6.30	9.74	9.02	8.30	8.61
Bhatinda	9.25	9.01	10.10	8.67	7.82	8.26	6.83	7.40	8.57	9.57	10.57	9.48
Ferozepur	5.66	5.59	7.59	7.75	6.60	5.59	4.46	6.48	7.04	8.08	9.11	8.41
Gurdaspur	..	6.10	..	5.78	3.88	4.78	3.95	3.37	6.64	6.90	7.16	6.83
Gurgaon	7.62	5.19	4.89	5.37	5.41	4.94	3.62	5.39	6.32	6.42	6.71	6.50
Hissar	9.37	11.46	9.66	7.15	..	11.72	4.79	8.55	7.14	7.93	10.68	9.91
Hoshiarpur	5.29	5.15	5.93	5.78	5.43	4.79	5.95	4.83	5.76	6.78	7.81	7.42
Jullundur	5.60	6.39	7.36	6.94	5.65	4.89	4.17	5.61	6.74	7.21	7.68	8.91
Kapurthala	..	..	10.40	9.25	8.80	7.06	6.63	7.68	8.10	8.90	9.70	9.16
Karnal	4.68	3.58	5.14	5.37	4.03	3.86	2.58	5.50	5.68	8.35	9.39	8.27
Ludhiana	6.61	6.64	6.50	6.64	7.14	6.50	6.37	7.52	6.22	7.92	9.63	9.63
M. Garh	9.93	8.06	7.44	8.59	5.03	5.93	5.51	4.04	4.00	5.87	6.98	6.28
Rohtak	..	7.78	8.37	6.44	6.94	5.32	3.62	5.39	6.95	7.71	8.05	8.42
Sangrur	8.86	9.01	9.96	8.09	7.63	7.25	7.33	8.36	8.76	8.28	7.81	8.70
Panjab	7.25	6.61	7.18	6.34	5.92	5.96	5.33	6.14	7.50	8.06	8.62	8.57
Haryana		6.61	7.18	6.34	5.92	5.05	4.12	5.83	6.35	7.39	8.27	7.97

Table A.15: Agricultural Wages in Kgs. of Wheat per Day in Panjab and Haryana 1961 to 1972 (Agr. Year) (Harvesting)

District	1960/1	1961/2	1962/3	1963/4	1964/5	1965/6	1966/7	1967/8	1968/9	1969/70	1970/1	1971/2
Ambala	8.18	5.19	9.03	9.66	8.60	5.51	..	4.93	5.68	6.42	7.04	7.31
Amritsar	..	..	..	..	5.65	5.59	7.01	8.97	11.94	10.74	8.55	8.32
Bhatinda	..	12.87	10.40	12.72	10.37	7.99	6.79	8.85	14.70	11.91	9.11	12.74
Ferozepur	5.29	5.15	5.20	8.67	11.31	5.99	5.56	12.96	10.41	11.71	13.01	11.56
Gurdaspur	7.35	..	..	..	..	6.39	3.98	3.87	..	6.73	7.63	7.74
Gurgaon	7.81	6.43	5.65	4.74	4.20	4.72	3.88	5.39	5.27	6.85	6.71	6.28
Hissar	8.34	10.81	9.37	9.66	..	..	5.17	6.28	5.79	7.62	12.61	8.71
Hoshiarpur	5.29	5.15	5.98	5.25	6.45	4.79	3.82	6.01	8.01	8.92	9.76	10.19
Jullundur	6.93	7.08	6.81	8.09	5.65	..	..	..	6.74	7.52	19.11	10.44
Kapurthala	..	..	..	13.88	8.95	7.59	..	..	6.74	8.05	9.61	11.46
Karnal	..	..	..	3.22	3.82	..	5.17	6.12	7.06	9.43	14.76	8.03
Ludhiana	8.80	7.47	7.44	6.94	7.26	..	6.37	8.10	8.36	11.99	15.62	11.04
M. Garh	9.37	6.48	..	..	..	..	..	5.13	4.69	5.14	6.71	6.28
Rohtak	..	9.57	8.81	8.05	..	5.51	3.10	6.47	9.41	10.92	11.40	8.33
Sangrur	6.61	8.60	9.96	10.41	7.69	7.19	8.28	7.78	8.57	8.84	9.11	10.95
Panjab	..	..	..	..	..	6.29	6.28	7.96	9.10	9.72	10.33	10.49
Haryana	7.10	7.24	7.26	8.04	6.87	5.24	4.70	6.46	6.25	7.98	9.71	7.50

Table A.16: Agricultural Wages in Kgs. of Wheat per Day in Panjab and Haryana 1961 to 1972
(Agr. Year)   (Weeding)

District	1960/1	1961/2	1962/3	1963/4	1964/5	1965/6	1966/7	1967/8	1968/9	1969/70	1970/1	1971/2
Ambala	7.93	7.18	6.63	6.44	5.62	5.51	..	5.39	5.51	6.42	6.71	7.33
Amritsar	5.29	5.15	4.45	5.78	6.07	5.54	5.20	6.30	8.57	8.48	8.38	8.71
Bhatinda	9.52	8.88	8.84	8.67	8.07	7.50	6.58	7.40	7.96	9.03	10.09	9.46
Ferozepur	7.93	7.83	7.80	7.91	6.09	5.59	4.68	5.44	7.14	8.13	9.11	8.37
Gurdaspur	..	..	..	..	4.94	..	3.77	3.47	6.26	6.76	7.16	6.76
Gurgaon	6.78	5.83	5.50	4.66	4.36	4.72	3.79	4.20	4.65	5.14	5.75	6.17
Hissar	7.25	9.83	9.37	8.59	6.21	4.72	3.50	5.72	6.64	7.32	9.60	7.85
Hoshiarpur	..	..	6.06	5.78	5.18	4.79	3.82	3.98	5.41	7.26	9.11	7.42
Jullundur	5.71	6.93	7.72	6.96	5.65	4.79	4.17	5.66	6.74	7.28	7.81	8.91
Kapurthala	..	7.72	..	9.25	7.18	5.94	5.51	7.31	6.48	7.47	8.46	9.16
Karnal	4.37	2.88	3.67	3.22	3.06	4.03	2.58	4.04	3.95	5.46	6.71	6.60
Ludhiana	6.42	6.51	6.97	7.33	6.84	6.39	5.73	6.95	6.74	8.18	9.63	9.35
M. Garh	..	5.19	..	..	3.82	4.33	4.13	4.04	3.70	5.39	6.71	6.28
Rohtak	..	8.22	7.34	6.44	6.50	4.88	3.10	4.71	6.03	7.06	7.39	6.91
Sangrur	6.71	8.81	9.75	8.09	7.65	7.19	6.37	7.71	8.76	8.12	7.48	8.76
Panjab	6.24	6.72	6.53	6.52	5.78	5.85	5.02	5.95	7.14	7.83	8.52	8.56
Haryana	..	..	..	..	..	4.69	3.83	5.05	5.36	6.22	7.08	6.86

Table A.17: Agricultural Wages in Kgs. of Wheat per Day in Panjab and Haryana 1961 to 1972
(Agr. Year)   (Other Agricultural Operations)

District	1960/1	1961/2	1962/3	1963/4	1964/5	1965/6	1966/7	1967/8	1968/9	1969/70	1970/1	1971/2
Ambala	6.25	5.24	6.63	6.12	5.41	5.51	3.10	5.51	6.11	6.42	6.71	7.23
Amritsar	6.50	6.26	4.65	6.01	6.26	5.67	5.24	6.38	10.40	9.40	8.39	8.43
Bhatinda	9.57	8.83	9.33	8.09	8.48	7.51	6.51	7.40	8.06	8.96	9.86	9.72
Ferozepur	5.29	7.29	5.20	..	5.90	5.59	4.46	5.18	7.07	8.20	9.33	8.57
Gurdaspur	..	3.86	..	..	3.11	..	3.71	3.51	5.78	6.47	7.16	6.85
Gurgaon	6.25	5.19	4.89	4.83	4.15	4.66	4.33	5.95	6.09	6.42	6.71	6.28
Hissar	7.81	10.55	9.37	7.88	5.47	3.86	3.95	6.86	5.78	7.71	10.23	8.92
Hoshiarpur	..	..	..	..	5.65	4.79	..	..	4.90	6.36	7.81	7.32
Jullundur	6.58	7.52	7.75	7.52	5.65	4.79	4.24	5.68	6.74	7.19	7.64	8.91
Kapurthala	..	..	..	..	..	4.79	..	..	6.94	7.86	8.78	9.55
Karnal	6.25	5.34	6.12	5.37	4.78	3.84	2.58	4.53	5.31	7.32	8.16	8.50
Ludhiana	6.26	6.18	6.63	5.78	4.86	5.59	5.90	7.45	7.20	8.33	9.46	9.30
M. Garh	..	6.74	6.43	6.44	5.73	7.55	3.96	6.29	5.05	5.36	6.89	6.20
Rohtak	..	7.78	7.34	7.51	5.98	4.56	3.10	4.71	5.68	6.42	7.38	4.90
Sangrur	..	10.30	6.16	..	6.46	6.07	6.46	6.75	8.57	8.19	7.81	8.76
Panjab	6.53	6.74	6.35	6.48	5.39	5.61	5.28	6.10	7.31	7.06	8.41	8.61
Haryana						5.04	3.67	5.63	5.58	6.64	7.93	7.18

INDEX

Adamski, I. 85
Adelman, I. 85
agricultural extension 3, 81
  economic evaluation of 81–2
  regression model of 26
  rural education and 81
agricultural labour
  demand curve 62–3
  occupation classification 60
  supply curve 62
agricultural produce
  gross value of (GAP) 45–9
  growth rate in 21
agricultural productivity
  educational inputs and 78, 80
  level of technology 1, 2
  marginal productivity principles 10
  productivity equations 17
  rate of return 10–11
  response uncertainty 2
  theory of production 10–13
  tubewells and 41, 44
  worker education in 80, 81
agricultural sector
  Haryana 9ff
  Panjab 9ff
  wheat, area sown 41
agricultural workers
  census figures 61
  cultivators 60–1, (see also farmers)
  differences, educational 7
  entrepreneurs 15
  farmer's entrepreneurial skills 8,
    10, 14–16
  farm workers 60
  income differential 11
  labourers 60–1
  lack of education 23
  literacy 23
  management decisions 7–8
  occupation classification 60
  performance of 7–8
  self-employed 10
  worker skills 10
agriculture
  Credit Co-op in 6
  fertiliser use in 21
  input factors 3–6

  tradable 20
  non-tradable 14
  marketing Co-op in 6
  tractorisation 21, 63
Ardito-Barleta, N. 85
Arrow 3

Bailey 9ff
Becker, G. S. 10
Bell, Clive 4
Bessell, J. E. 86
Bos, H. C. 13
Brown 19ff
Butler, M. 104

Castillo, G. 87
causal chain 41–9
census (1961, 1971) 21, 23, 26, 60,
    61, 62
change, technical 3
Chaudhri, D. P. 9ff, 10, 13, 15, 19ff,
    28, 69, 80, 87–8
Chow test 36
Cobb-Douglas production function 51
coefficient of education 36, 54, 56,
    66, 67
  caste factors in 56
  worker effect in 54, 56
co-operative credit 38–9, 48
Correa, H. 13
correlation coefficient 24, 42, 52, 64
cost-benefit analysis 68–70
cost-benefit ratio 69
crop husbandry practices 46
cross-section data 36
cultivating households 51, 54
cultivators (see agricultural workers)

Dandekar, V. M. 88
Dasgupta, Biplah 9ff
decisions
  allocative 7–8, 18, 20
  management 7–8
development, agricultural 1
differences, educational 7
double cropping 6
dualism, economic 2–3